You Don't Know JS: ES6 and Beyond

Kyle Simpson

Beijing · Boston · Farnham · Sebastopol · Tokyo

You Don't Know JS: ES6 & Beyond

by Kyle Simpson

Copyright © 2016 Getify Solutions, Inc. All rights reserved.

Printed in the United States of America.

Published by O'Reilly Media, Inc., 1005 Gravenstein Highway North, Sebastopol, CA 95472.

O'Reilly books may be purchased for educational, business, or sales promotional use. Online editions are also available for most titles (*http://safaribooksonline.com*). For more information, contact our corporate/institutional sales department: 800-998-9938 or *corporate@oreilly.com*.

Editors: Simon St. Laurent and Brian MacDonald	**Proofreader:** Christina Edwards
Production Editor: Kristen Brown	**Interior Designer:** David Futato
Copyeditor: Jasmine Kwityn	**Cover Designer:** Randy Comer
	Illustrator: Rebecca Demarest

January 2016: First Edition

Revision History for the First Edition
2015-12-11: First Release

See *http://oreilly.com/catalog/errata.csp?isbn=9781491904244* for release details.

The O'Reilly logo is a registered trademark of O'Reilly Media, Inc. *You Don't Know JS: ES6 & Beyond*, the cover image, and related trade dress are trademarks of O'Reilly Media, Inc.

978-1-491-90424-4

[LSI]

Table of Contents

Foreword

Kyle Simpson is a thorough pragmatist.

I can't think of higher praise than this. To me, these are two of the most important qualities that a software developer must have. That's right: *must*, not *should*. Kyle's keen ability to tease apart layers of the JavaScript programming language and present them in understandable and meaningful portions is second to none.

ES6 & Beyond will be familiar to readers of the *You Don't Know JS* series: they can expect to be deeply immersed in everything from the obvious, to the very subtle—revealing semantics that were either taken for granted or never even considered. Until now, the *You Don't Know JS* book series has covered material that has at least some degree of familiarity to its readers. They have either seen or heard about the subject matter; they may even have experience with it. This volume covers material that only a very small portion of the JavaScript developer community has been exposed to: the evolutionary changes to the language introduced in the ECMAScript 2015 Language Specification.

Over the last couple years, I've witnessed Kyle's tireless efforts to familiarize himself with this material to a level of expertise that is rivaled by only a handful of his professional peers. That's quite a feat, considering that at the time of this writing, the language specification document hasn't been formally published! But what I've said is true, and I've read every word that Kyle's written for this book. I've followed every change, and each time, the content only gets better and provides yet a deeper level of understanding.

This book is about shaking up your sense of understanding by exposing you to the new and unknown. The intention is to evolve your knowledge in step with your tools by bestowing you with new capabilities. It exists to give you the confidence to fully embrace the next major era of JavaScript programming.

—Rick Waldron (@rwaldron),
Open Web Engineer at Bocoup
Ecma/TC39 Representative
for jQuery

Preface

I'm sure you noticed, but "JS" in the series title is not an abbreviation for words used to curse about JavaScript, though cursing at the language's quirks is something we can probably all identify with!

From the earliest days of the Web, JavaScript has been a foundational technology that drives interactive experience around the content we consume. While flickering mouse trails and annoying pop-up prompts may be where JavaScript started, nearly two decades later, the technology and capability of JavaScript has grown many orders of magnitude, and few doubt its importance at the heart of the world's most widely available software platform: the Web.

But as a language, it has perpetually been a target for a great deal of criticism, owing partly to its heritage but even more to its design philosophy. Even the name evokes, as Brendan Eich once put it, "dumb kid brother" status next to its more mature older brother Java. But the name is merely an accident of politics and marketing. The two languages are vastly different in many important ways. "JavaScript" is as related to "Java" as "Carnival" is to "Car."

Because JavaScript borrows concepts and syntax idioms from several languages, including proud C-style procedural roots as well as subtle, less obvious Scheme/Lisp-style functional roots, it is exceedingly approachable to a broad audience of developers, even those with little to no programming experience. The "Hello World" of JavaScript is so simple that the language is inviting and easy to get comfortable with in early exposure.

While JavaScript is perhaps one of the easiest languages to get up and running with, its eccentricities make solid mastery of the language a vastly less common occurrence than in many other languages. Where it takes a pretty in-depth knowledge of a language like C or C++ to write a full-scale program, full-scale production JavaScript can, and often does, barely scratch the surface of what the language can do.

Sophisticated concepts that are deeply rooted into the language tend instead to surface themselves in *seemingly* simplistic ways, such as passing around functions as callbacks, which encourages the JavaScript developer to just use the language as-is and not worry too much about what's going on under the hood.

It is simultaneously a simple, easy-to-use language that has broad appeal, and a complex and nuanced collection of language mechanics that without careful study will elude *true understanding* even for the most seasoned of JavaScript developers.

Therein lies the paradox of JavaScript, the Achilles' heel of the language, the challenge we are presently addressing. Because JavaScript *can* be used without understanding, the understanding of the language is often never attained.

Mission

If at every point that you encounter a surprise or frustration in JavaScript, your response is to add it to the blacklist (as some are accustomed to doing), you soon will be relegated to a hollow shell of the richness of JavaScript.

While this subset has been famously dubbed "The Good Parts," I would implore you, dear reader, to instead consider it the "The Easy Parts," "The Safe Parts," or even "The Incomplete Parts."

This *You Don't Know JS* series offers a contrary challenge: learn and deeply understand *all* of JavaScript, even and especially "The Tough Parts."

Here, we address head-on the tendency of JS developers to learn "just enough" to get by, without ever forcing themselves to learn exactly how and why the language behaves the way it does. Furthermore, we eschew the common advice to retreat when the road gets rough.

I am not content, nor should you be, at stopping once something just works and not really knowing *why*. I gently challenge you to journey down that bumpy "road less traveled" and embrace all that JavaScript is and can do. With that knowledge, no technique, no framework, no popular buzzword acronym of the week will be beyond your understanding.

These books each take on specific core parts of the language that are most commonly misunderstood or under-understood, and dive very deep and exhaustively into them. You should come away from reading with a firm confidence in your understanding, not just of the theoretical, but the practical "what you need to know" bits.

The JavaScript you know right now is probably parts handed down to you by others who've been burned by incomplete understanding. *That* JavaScript is but a shadow of the true language. You don't really know JavaScript *yet*, but if you dig into this series, you will. Read on, my friends. JavaScript awaits you.

Review

JavaScript is awesome. It's easy to learn partially, and much harder to learn completely (or even *sufficiently*). When developers encounter confusion, they usually blame the language instead of their lack of understanding. These books aim to fix that, inspiring a strong appreciation for the language you can now, and *should*, deeply know.

 Many of the examples in this book assume modern (and future-reaching) JavaScript engine environments, such as ES6. Some code may not work as described if run in older (pre-ES6) engines.

Conventions Used in This Book

The following typographical conventions are used in this book:

Italic
> Indicates new terms, URLs, email addresses, filenames, and file extensions.

Constant width

Used for program listings, as well as within paragraphs to refer to program elements such as variable or function names, databases, data types, environment variables, statements, and keywords.

Constant width bold

Shows commands or other text that should be typed literally by the user.

Constant width italic

Shows text that should be replaced with user-supplied values or by values determined by context.

This element signifies a tip or suggestion.

This element signifies a general note.

This element indicates a warning or caution.

Using Code Examples

Supplemental material (code examples, exercises, etc.) is available for download at *http://bit.ly/ydkjs-es6beyond-code*.

This book is here to help you get your job done. In general, if example code is offered with this book, you may use it in your programs and documentation. You do not need to contact us for permission unless you're reproducing a significant portion of the code. For example, writing a program that uses several chunks of code from this book does not require permission. Selling or distributing a CD-ROM of examples from O'Reilly books does require permission. Answering a question by citing this book and quoting example code does not require permission. Incorporating a significant amount of example code from this book into your product's documentation does require permission.

We appreciate, but do not require, attribution. An attribution usually includes the title, author, publisher, and ISBN. For example: "*You Don't Know JavaScript: ES6 & Beyond* by Kyle Simpson (O'Reilly). Copyright 2016 Getify Solutions, Inc., 978-1-491-90424-4."

If you feel your use of code examples falls outside fair use or the permission given above, feel free to contact us at *permissions@oreilly.com*.

Safari® Books Online

 *Safari Books Online* is an on-demand digital library that delivers expert content in both book and video form from the world's leading authors in technology and business.

Technology professionals, software developers, web designers, and business and creative professionals use Safari Books Online as their primary resource for research, problem solving, learning, and certification training.

Safari Books Online offers a range of plans and pricing for enterprise, government, education, and individuals.

Members have access to thousands of books, training videos, and prepublication manuscripts in one fully searchable database from publishers like O'Reilly Media, Prentice Hall Professional, Addison-Wesley Professional, Microsoft Press, Sams, Que, Peachpit Press, Focal Press, Cisco Press, John Wiley & Sons, Syngress, Morgan Kaufmann, IBM Redbooks, Packt, Adobe Press, FT Press, Apress, Manning, New Riders, McGraw-Hill, Jones & Bartlett, Course Technology, and hundreds more. For more information about Safari Books Online, please visit us online.

How to Contact Us

Please address comments and questions concerning this book to the publisher:

O'Reilly Media, Inc.
1005 Gravenstein Highway North
Sebastopol, CA 95472
800-998-9938 (in the United States or Canada)
707-829-0515 (international or local)
707-829-0104 (fax)

We have a web page for this book, where we list errata, examples, and any additional information. You can access this page at *http://bit.ly/ydkjs-es6-beyond*.

To comment or ask technical questions about this book, send email to *bookquestions@oreilly.com*.

For more information about our books, courses, conferences, and news, see our website at *http://www.oreilly.com*.

Find us on Facebook: *http://facebook.com/oreilly*

Follow us on Twitter: *http://twitter.com/oreillymedia*

Watch us on YouTube: *http://www.youtube.com/oreillymedia*

CHAPTER 1

ES? Now & Future

Before you dive into this book, you should have a solid working proficiency over JavaScript up to the most recent standard (at the time of this writing), which is commonly called *ES5* (technically ES 5.1). Here, we plan to talk squarely about the upcoming *ES6*, as well as cast our vision beyond to understand how JS will evolve moving forward.

If you are still looking for confidence with JavaScript, I highly recommend you read the other titles in this series first:

- *Up & Going*: Are you new to programming and JS? This is the roadmap you need to consult as you start your learning journey.

- *Scope & Closures*: Did you know that JS lexical scope is based on compiler (not interpreter!) semantics? Can you explain how closures are a direct result of lexical scope and functions as values?

- *this & Object Prototypes*: Can you recite the four simple rules for how this is bound? Have you been muddling through fake "classes" in JS instead of adopting the simpler "behavior delegation" design pattern? Ever heard of *objects linked to other objects* (OLOO)?

- *Types & Grammar*: Do you know the built-in types in JS, and more importantly, do you know how to properly and safely use coercion between types? How comfortable are you with the nuances of JS grammar/syntax?

- *Async & Performance*: Are you still using callbacks to manage your asynchrony? Can you explain what a promise is and why/how it solves "callback hell"? Do you know how to use generators to improve the legibility of async code? What exactly constitutes mature optimization of JS programs and individual operations?

If you've already read all those titles and you feel pretty comfortable with the topics they cover, it's time we dive into the evolution of JS to explore all the changes coming not only soon but farther over the horizon.

Unlike ES5, ES6 is not just a modest set of new APIs added to the language. It incorporates a whole slew of new syntactic forms, some of which may take quite a bit of getting used to. There's also a variety of new organization forms and new API helpers for various data types.

ES6 is a radical jump forward for the language. Even if you think you know JS in ES5, ES6 is full of new stuff you *don't know yet*, so get ready! This book explores all the major themes of ES6 that you need to get up to speed on, and even gives you a glimpse of future features coming down the track that you should be aware of.

 All code in this book assumes an ES6+ environment. At the time of this writing, ES6 support varies quite a bit in browsers and JS environments (like Node.js), so your mileage may vary.

Versioning

The JavaScript standard is referred to officially as "ECMAScript" (abbreviated "ES"), and up until just recently has been versioned entirely by ordinal number (i.e., "5" for "5th edition").

The earliest versions, ES1 and ES2, were not widely known or implemented. ES3 was the first widespread baseline for JavaScript, and constitutes the JavaScript standard for browsers like IE6-8 and older Android 2.x mobile browsers. For political reasons beyond what we'll cover here, the ill-fated ES4 never came about.

In 2009, ES5 was officially finalized (later ES5.1 in 2011), and settled as the widespread standard for JS for the modern revolution and explosion of browsers, such as Firefox, Chrome, Opera, Safari, and many others.

Leading up to the expected *next* version of JS (slipped from 2013 to 2014 and then 2015), the obvious and common label in discourse has been ES6.

However, late into the ES6 specification timeline, suggestions have surfaced that versioning may in the future switch to a year-based schema, such as ES2016 (aka ES7) to refer to whatever version of the specification is finalized before the end of 2016. Some disagree, but ES6 will likely maintain its dominant mindshare over the late-change substitute ES2015. However, ES2016 may in fact signal the new year-based schema.

It has also been observed that the pace of JS evolution is much faster even than single-year versioning. As soon as an idea begins to progress through standards discussions, browsers start prototyping the feature, and early adopters start experimenting with the code.

Usually well before there's an official stamp of approval, a feature is de facto standardized by virtue of this early engine/tooling prototyping. So it's also valid to consider the future of JS versioning to be per-feature rather than per-arbitrary-collection-of-major-features (as it is now) or even per-year (as it may become).

The takeaway is that the version labels stop being as important, and JavaScript starts to be seen more as an evergreen, living standard. The best way to cope with this is to stop thinking about your code base as being "ES6-based," for instance, and instead consider it feature by feature for support.

Transpiling

Made even worse by the rapid evolution of features, a problem arises for JS developers who at once may both strongly desire to use new features while at the same time being slapped with the reality that their sites/apps may need to support older browsers without such support.

The way ES5 appears to have played out in the broader industry, the typical mindset was that code bases waited to adopt ES5 until most if not all pre-ES5 environments had fallen out of their support spectrum. As a result, many are just recently (at the time of this writing) starting to adopt things like `strict` mode, which landed in ES5 over five years ago.

It's widely considered to be a harmful approach for the future of the JS ecosystem to wait around and trail the specification by so many years. All those responsible for evolving the language desire for developers to begin basing their code on the new features and patterns as soon as they stabilize in specification form and browsers have a chance to implement them.

So how do we resolve this seeming contradiction? The answer is tooling, specifically a technique called *transpiling* (transformation + compiling). Roughly, the idea is to use a special tool to transform your ES6 code into equivalent (or close!) matches that work in ES5 environments.

For example, consider shorthand property definitions (see "Object Literal Extensions" on page 38 in Chapter 2). Here's the ES6 form:

```
var foo = [1,2,3];

var obj = {
    foo     // means `foo: foo`
};

obj.foo;    // [1,2,3]
```

But (roughly) here's how that transpiles:

```
var foo = [1,2,3];

var obj = {
    foo: foo
};

obj.foo;    // [1,2,3]
```

This is a minor but pleasant transformation that lets us shorten the foo: foo in an object literal declaration to just foo, if the names are the same.

Transpilers perform these transformations for you, usually in a build workflow step similar to how you perform linting, minification, and other similar operations.

Shims/Polyfills

Not all new ES6 features need a transpiler. Polyfills (aka shims) are a pattern for defining equivalent behavior from a newer environment into an older environment, when possible. Syntax cannot be polyfilled, but APIs often can be.

For example, `Object.is(..)` is a new utility for checking strict equality of two values but without the nuanced exceptions that `===` has for `NaN` and `-0` values. The polyfill for `Object.is(..)` is pretty easy:

```
if (!Object.is) {
    Object.is = function(v1, v2) {
        // test for `-0`
        if (v1 === 0 && v2 === 0) {
            return 1 / v1 === 1 / v2;
        }
        // test for `NaN`
        if (v1 !== v1) {
            return v2 !== v2;
        }
        // everything else
        return v1 === v2;
    };
}
```

Pay attention to the outer `if` statement guard wrapped around the polyfill. This is an important detail, which means the snippet only defines its fallback behavior for older environments where the API in question isn't already defined; it would be very rare that you'd want to overwrite an existing API.

There's a great collection of ES6 shims called "ES6 Shim" (*https://github.com/paulmillr/es6-shim/*) that you should definitely adopt as a standard part of any new JS project!

It is assumed that JS will continue to evolve constantly, with browsers rolling out support for features continually rather than in large chunks. So the best strategy for keeping updated as it evolves is to just introduce polyfill shims into your code base, and a transpiler step into your build workflow, right now and get used to that new reality.

If you decide to keep the status quo and just wait around for all browsers without a feature supported to go away before you start using the feature, you're always going to be way behind. You'll sadly be missing out on all the innovations designed to make writing JavaScript more effective, efficient, and robust.

Review

ES6 (some may try to call it ES2015) is just landing as of the time of this writing, and it has lots of new stuff you need to learn!

But it's even more important to shift your mindset to align with the new way that JavaScript is going to evolve. It's not just waiting around for years for some official document to get a vote of approval, as many have done in the past.

Now, JavaScript features land in browsers as they become ready, and it's up to you whether you'll get on the train early or whether you'll be playing costly catch-up games years from now.

Whatever labels that future JavaScript adopts, it's going to move a lot quicker than it ever has before. Transpilers and shims/polyfills are important tools to keep you on the forefront of where the language is headed.

If there's any narrative important to understand about the new reality for JavaScript, it's that all JS developers are strongly implored to move from the trailing edge of the curve to the leading edge. And learning ES6 is where that all starts!

CHAPTER 2

Syntax

If you've been writing JS for any length of time, odds are the syntax is pretty familiar to you. There are certainly many quirks, but overall it's a fairly reasonable and straightforward syntax that draws many similarities from other languages.

However, ES6 adds quite a few new syntactic forms that take some getting used to. In this chapter, we'll tour through them to find out what's in store.

At the time of this writing, some of the features discussed in this book have been implemented in various browsers (Firefox, Chrome, etc.), but some have only been partially implemented and many others have not been implemented at all. Your experience may be mixed trying these examples directly. If so, try them out with tran‐spilers, as most of these features are covered by those tools.

ES6Fiddle (*http://www.es6fiddle.net/*) is a great, easy-to-use playground for trying out ES6, as is the online REPL for the Babel transpiler (*http://babeljs.io/repl/*).

Block-Scoped Declarations

You're probably aware that the fundamental unit of variable scoping in JavaScript has always been the `function`. If you needed to create a block of scope, the most prevalent way to do so other than a regular function declaration was the immediately invoked function expression (IIFE). For example:

```
var a = 2;

(function IIFE(){
    var a = 3;
    console.log( a );    // 3
})();

console.log( a );        // 2
```

let Declarations

However, we can now create declarations that are bound to any block, called (unsurprisingly) *block scoping*. This means all we need is a pair of { .. } to create a scope. Instead of using var, which always declares variables attached to the enclosing function (or global, if top level) scope, use let:

```
var a = 2;

{
    let a = 3;
    console.log( a );    // 3
}

console.log( a );        // 2
```

It's not very common or idiomatic thus far in JS to use a standalone { .. } block, but it's always been valid. And developers from other languages that have *block scoping* will readily recognize that pattern.

I believe this is the best way to create block-scoped variables, with a dedicated { .. } block. Moreover, you should always put the let declaration(s) at the very top of that block. If you have more than one to declare, I'd recommend using just one let.

Stylistically, I even prefer to put the let on the same line as the opening {, to make it clearer that this block is only for the purpose of declaring the scope for those variables.

```
{   let a = 2, b, c;
    // ..
}
```

Now, that's going to look strange and it's not likely going to match the recommendations given in most other ES6 literature. But I have reasons for my madness.

There's another experimental (not standardized) form of the `let` declaration called the `let`-block, which looks like:

```
let (a = 2, b, c) {
    // ..
}
```

That form is what I call *explicit* block scoping, whereas the `let` .. declaration form that mirrors `var` is more *implicit*, as it kind of hijacks whatever { .. } pair it's found in. Generally developers find *explicit* mechanisms a bit more preferable than *implicit* mechanisms, and I claim this is one of those cases.

If you compare the previous two snippet forms, they're very similar, and in my opinion both qualify stylistically as *explicit* block scoping. Unfortunately, the `let` (..) { .. } form, the most *explicit* of the options, was not adopted in ES6. That may be revisited post-ES6, but for now the former option is our best bet, I think.

To reinforce the *implicit* nature of `let` .. declarations, consider these usages:

```
let a = 2;

if (a > 1) {
    let b = a * 3;
    console.log( b );        // 6

    for (let i = a; i <= b; i++) {
        let j = i + 10;
        console.log( j );
    }
    // 12 13 14 15 16

    let c = a + b;
    console.log( c );        // 8
}
```

Quick quiz without looking back at that snippet: which variable(s) exist only inside the `if` statement, and which variable(s) exist only inside the `for` loop?

The answers: the `if` statement contains b and c block-scoped variables, and the `for` loop contains i and j block-scoped variables.

Did you have to think about it for a moment? Does it surprise you that i isn't added to the enclosing if statement scope? That mental pause and questioning—I call it a "mental tax"—comes from the fact that this let mechanism is not only new to us, but it's also *implicit*.

There's also a hazard in the let c = .. declaration appearing so far down in the scope. Unlike traditional var-declared variables, which are attached to the entire enclosing function scope regardless of where they appear, let declarations attach to the block scope but are not initialized until they appear in the block.

Accessing a let-declared variable earlier than its let .. declaration/initialization causes an error, whereas with var declarations the ordering doesn't matter (except stylistically).

Consider:

```
{
    console.log( a );   // undefined
    console.log( b );   // ReferenceError!

    var a;
    let b;
}
```

This ReferenceError from accessing too-early let-declared references is technically called a *Temporal Dead Zone (TDZ)* error—you're accessing a variable that's been declared but not yet initialized. This will not be the only time we see TDZ errors—they crop up in several places in ES6. Also, note that "initialized" doesn't require explicitly assigning a value in your code, as let b; is totally valid. A variable that's not given an assignment at declaration time is assumed to have been assigned the undefined value, so let b; is the same as let b = undefined;. Explicit assignment or not, you cannot access b until the let b statement is run.

One last gotcha: typeof behaves differently with TDZ variables than it does with undeclared (or declared!) variables. For example:

```
{
    // `a` is not declared
    if (typeof a === "undefined") {
```

```
        console.log( "cool" );
    }

    // `b` is declared, but in its TDZ
    if (typeof b === "undefined") {      // ReferenceError!
        // ..
    }

    // ..

    let b;
}
```

The a is not declared, so `typeof` is the only safe way to check for its existence or not. But `typeof` b throws the TDZ error because farther down in the code there happens to be a `let` b declaration. Oops.

Now it should be clearer why I insist that `let` declarations should all be at the top of their scope. That totally avoids the accidental errors of accessing too early. It also makes it more *explicit* when you look at the start of a block, any block, what variables it contains.

Your blocks (`if` statements, `while` loops, etc.) don't have to share their original behavior with scoping behavior.

This explicitness on your part, which is up to you to maintain with discipline, will save you lots of refactor headaches and footguns down the line.

For more information on `let` and block scoping, see Chapter 3 of the *Scope & Closures* title of this series.

let + for

The only exception I'd make to the preference for the *explicit* form of `let` declaration blocking is a `let` that appears in the header of a `for` loop. The reason may seem nuanced, but I believe it to be one of the more important ES6 features.

Consider:

```
var funcs = [];

for (let i = 0; i < 5; i++) {
```

```
        funcs.push( function(){
            console.log( i );
        } );
    }

funcs[3]();     // 3
```

The `let i` in the `for` header declares an `i` not just for the `for` loop itself, but it redeclares a new `i` for each iteration of the loop. That means that closures created inside the loop iteration close over those per-iteration variables the way you'd expect.

If you tried that same snippet but with `var i` in the `for` loop header, you'd get 5 instead of 3, because there'd only be one `i` in the outer scope that was closed over, instead of a new `i` for each iteration's function to close over.

You could also have accomplished the same thing slightly more verbosely:

```
var funcs = [];

for (var i = 0; i < 5; i++) {
    let j = i;
    funcs.push( function(){
        console.log( j );
    } );
}

funcs[3]();     // 3
```

Here, we forcibly create a new `j` for each iteration, and then the closure works the same way. I prefer the former approach; that extra special capability is why I endorse the `for (let .. ) ..` form. It could be argued that it's somewhat more *implicit*, but it's *explicit* enough, and useful enough, for my tastes.

`let` also works the same way with `for..in` and `for..of` loops (see "for..of Loops" on page 61).

const Declarations

There's one other form of block-scoped declaration to consider: the `const`, which creates *constants*.

What exactly is a constant? It's a variable that's read-only after its initial value is set. Consider:

```
{
    const a = 2;
    console.log( a );    // 2

    a = 3;               // TypeError!
}
```

You are not allowed to change the value the variable holds once it's been set, at declaration time. A const declaration must have an explicit initialization. If you wanted a *constant* with the undefined value, you'd have to declare const a = undefined to get it.

Constants are not a restriction on the value itself, but on the variable's assignment of that value. In other words, the value is not frozen or immutable because of const, just the assignment of it. If the value is complex, such as an object or array, the contents of the value can still be modified:

```
{
    const a = [1,2,3];
    a.push( 4 );
    console.log( a );    // [1,2,3,4]

    a = 42;              // TypeError!
}
```

The a variable doesn't actually hold a constant array; rather, it holds a constant reference to the array. The array itself is freely mutable.

 Assigning an object or array as a constant means that value will not be able to be garbage collected until that constant's lexical scope goes away, as the reference to the value can never be unset. That may be desirable, but be careful if it's not your intent!

Essentially, const declarations enforce what we've stylistically signaled with our code for years, where we declared a variable name of all uppercase letters and assigned it some literal value that we took care never to change. There's no enforcement on a var assignment, but there is now with a const assignment, which can help you catch unintended changes.

const *can* be used with variable declarations of for, for..in, and for..of loops (see "for..of Loops" on page 61). However, an error will be thrown if there's any attempt to reassign, such as the typical i++ clause of a for loop.

const Or Not

There's some rumored assumptions that a const could be more optimizable by the JS engine in certain scenarios than a let or var would be. Theoretically, the engine more easily knows the variable's value/type will never change, so it can eliminate some possible tracking.

Whether const really helps here or this is just our own fantasies and intuitions, the much more important decision to make is if you intend constant behavior or not. Remember: one of the most important roles for source code is to communicate clearly, not only to you, but your future self and other code collaborators, what your intent is.

Some developers prefer to start out every variable declaration as a const and then relax a declaration back to a let if it becomes necessary for its value to change in the code. This is an interesting perspective, but it's not clear that it genuinely improves the readability or reason-ability of code.

It's not really a *protection*, as many believe, because any later developer who wants to change a value of a const can just blindly change const to let on the declaration. At best, it protects accidental change. But again, other than our intuitions and sensibilities, there doesn't appear to be an objective and clear measure of what constitutes "accidents" or prevention thereof. Similar mindsets exist around type enforcement.

My advice: to avoid potentially confusing code, only use const for variables that you're intentionally and obviously signaling will not change. In other words, don't *rely on* const for code behavior, but instead use it as a tool for signaling intent, when intent can be signaled clearly.

Block-Scoped Functions

Starting with ES6, function declarations that occur inside of blocks are now specified to be scoped to that block. Prior to ES6, the specification did not call for this, but many implementations did it anyway. So now the specification meets reality.

Consider:

```
{
    foo();                    // works!

    function foo() {
        // ..
    }
}

foo();                        // ReferenceError
```

The foo() function is declared inside the { .. } block, and as of ES6 is block-scoped there. So it's not available outside that block. But also note that it is "hoisted" within the block, as opposed to let declarations, which suffer the TDZ error trap mentioned earlier.

Block-scoping of function declarations could be a problem if you've ever written code like this before, and relied on the old legacy non-block-scoped behavior:

```
if (something) {
    function foo() {
        console.log( "1" );
    }
}
else {
    function foo() {
        console.log( "2" );
    }
}

foo();      // ??
```

In pre-ES6 environments, foo() would print "2" regardless of the value of something, because both function declarations were hoisted out of the blocks, and the second one always wins.

In ES6, that last line throws a ReferenceError.

Spread/Rest

ES6 introduces a new ... operator that's typically referred to as the *spread* or *rest* operator, depending on where/how it's used. Let's take a look:

```
function foo(x,y,z) {
    console.log( x, y, z );
}
```

```
foo( ...[1,2,3] );                // 1 2 3
```

When ... is used in front of an array (actually, any *iterable*, which we cover in Chapter 3), it acts to "spread" it out into its individual values.

You'll typically see that usage as is shown in that previous snippet, when spreading out an array as a set of arguments to a function call. In this usage, ... acts to give us a simpler syntactic replacement for the apply(..) method, which we would typically have used pre-ES6 as:

```
foo.apply( null, [1,2,3] );       // 1 2 3
```

But ... can be used to spread out/expand a value in other contexts as well, such as inside another array declaration:

```
var a = [2,3,4];
var b = [ 1, ...a, 5 ];

console.log( b );                 // [1,2,3,4,5]
```

In this usage, ... is basically replacing concat(..), as it behaves like [1].concat(a, [5]) here.

The other common usage of ... can be seen as essentially the opposite; instead of spreading a value out, the ... *gathers* a set of values together into an array. Consider:

```
function foo(x, y, ...z) {
    console.log( x, y, z );
}

foo( 1, 2, 3, 4, 5 );             // 1 2 [3,4,5]
```

The ...z in this snippet is essentially saying: "gather the *rest* of the arguments (if any) into an array called z." Because x was assigned 1, and y was assigned 2, the rest of the arguments 3, 4, and 5 were gathered into z.

Of course, if you don't have any named parameters, the ... gathers all arguments:

```
function foo(...args) {
    console.log( args );
}

foo( 1, 2, 3, 4, 5);              // [1,2,3,4,5]
```

The ...args in the foo(..) function declaration is usually called "rest parameters," because you're collecting the rest of the parameters. I prefer "gather," because it's more descriptive of what it does rather than what it contains.

The best part about this usage is that it provides a very solid alternative to using the long-since-deprecated arguments array—actually, it's not really an array, but an array-like object. Because args (or whatever you call it—a lot of people prefer r or rest) is a real array, we can get rid of lots of silly pre-ES6 tricks we jumped through to make arguments into something we can treat as an array.

Consider:

```
// doing things the new ES6 way
function foo(...args) {
    // `args` is already a real array

    // discard first element in `args`
    args.shift();

    // pass along all of `args` as arguments
    // to `console.log(..)`
    console.log( ...args );
}

// doing things the old-school pre-ES6 way
function bar() {
    // turn `arguments` into a real array
    var args = Array.prototype.slice.call( arguments );

    // add some elements on the end
    args.push( 4, 5 );

    // filter out odd numbers
    args = args.filter( function(v){
        return v % 2 == 0;
    } );

    // pass along all of `args` as arguments
    // to `foo(..)`
    foo.apply( null, args );
}

bar( 0, 1, 2, 3 );                    // 2 4
```

The ...args in the foo(..) function declaration gathers arguments, and the ...args in the console.log(..) call spreads them out.

That's a good illustration of the symmetric but opposite uses of the ... operator.

Besides the ... usage in a function declaration, there's another case where ... is used for gathering values, and we'll look at it in "Too Many, Too Few, Just Enough" on page 30 later in this chapter.

Default Parameter Values

Perhaps one of the most common idioms in JavaScript relates to setting a default value for a function parameter. The way we've done this for years should look quite familiar:

```
function foo(x,y) {
    x = x || 11;
    y = y || 31;

    console.log( x + y );
}

foo();              // 42
foo( 5, 6 );        // 11
foo( 5 );           // 36
foo( null, 6 );     // 17
```

Of course, if you've used this pattern before, you know that it's both helpful and a little bit dangerous if, for example, you need to be able to pass in what would otherwise be considered a falsy value for one of the parameters. Consider:

```
foo( 0, 42 );       // 53 <-- Oops, not 42
```

Why? Because the 0 is falsy, and so the x || 11 results in 11, not the directly passed in 0.

To fix this gotcha, some people will instead write the check more verbosely like this:

```
function foo(x,y) {
    x = (x !== undefined) ? x : 11;
    y = (y !== undefined) ? y : 31;

    console.log( x + y );
}

foo( 0, 42 );           // 42
foo( undefined, 6 );    // 17
```

Of course, that means any value except undefined can be directly passed in. However, undefined will be assumed to signal, "I didn't pass this in." That works great unless you actually need to be able to pass undefined in.

In that case, you could test to see if the argument is actually omitted, by it actually not being present in the arguments array, perhaps like this:

```
function foo(x,y) {
    x = (0 in arguments) ? x : 11;
    y = (1 in arguments) ? y : 31;

    console.log( x + y );
}

foo( 5 );                // 36
foo( 5, undefined );     // NaN
```

But how would you omit the first x argument without the ability to pass in any kind of value (not even undefined) that signals "I'm omitting this argument"?

foo(,5) is tempting, but it's invalid syntax. foo.apply(null,[,5]) seems like it should do the trick, but apply(..)'s quirks here mean the arguments are treated as [undefined,5], which of course doesn't omit.

If you investigate further, you'll find you can only omit arguments on the end (i.e., righthand side) by simply passing fewer arguments than "expected," but you cannot omit arguments in the middle or at the beginning of the arguments list. It's just not possible.

There's a principle applied to JavaScript's design here that is important to remember: undefined means *missing*. That is, there's no difference between undefined and *missing*, at least as far as function arguments go.

 There are, confusingly, other places in JS where this particular design principle doesn't apply, such as for arrays with empty slots. See the *Types & Grammar* title of this series for more information.

With all this in mind, we can now examine a nice helpful syntax added as of ES6 to streamline the assignment of default values to missing arguments:

```
function foo(x = 11, y = 31) {
    console.log( x + y );
}

foo();                  // 42
foo( 5, 6 );            // 11
foo( 0, 42 );           // 42

foo( 5 );               // 36
foo( 5, undefined );    // 36 <-- `undefined` is missing
foo( 5, null );         // 5  <-- null coerces to `0`

foo( undefined, 6 );    // 17 <-- `undefined` is missing
foo( null, 6 );         // 6  <-- null coerces to `0`
```

Notice the results and how they imply both subtle differences and similarities to the earlier approaches.

x = 11 in a function declaration is more like x !== undefined ? x : 11 than the much more common idiom x || 11, so you'll need to be careful in converting your pre-ES6 code to this ES6 default parameter value syntax.

 A rest/gather parameter (see "Spread/Rest" on page 15) cannot have a default value. So, while function foo(...vals=[1,2,3]) { might seem like an intriguing capability, it's not valid syntax. You'll need to continue to apply that sort of logic manually if necessary.

Default Value Expressions

Function default values can be more than just simple values like 31; they can be any valid expression, even a function call:

```
function bar(val) {
    console.log( "bar called!" );
    return y + val;
}

function foo(x = y + 3, z = bar( x )) {
    console.log( x, z );
}
```

```
var y = 5;
foo();                          // "bar called"
                                // 8 13
foo( 10 );                      // "bar called"
                                // 10 15

y = 6;
foo( undefined, 10 );           // 9 10
```

As you can see, the default value expressions are lazily evaluated, meaning they're only run if and when they're needed—that is, when a parameter's argument is omitted or is undefined.

It's a subtle detail, but the formal parameters in a function declaration are in their own scope (think of it as a scope bubble-wrapped around just the (..) of the function declaration), not in the function body's scope. That means a reference to an identifier in a default value expression first matches the formal parameters' scope before looking to an outer scope. See the *Scope & Closures* title of this series for more information.

Consider:

```
var w = 1, z = 2;

function foo( x = w + 1, y = x + 1, z = z + 1 ) {
    console.log( x, y, z );
}

foo();                          // ReferenceError
```

The w in the w + 1 default value expression looks for w in the formal parameters' scope, but does not find it, so the outer scope's w is used. Next, the x in the x + 1 default value expression finds x in the formal parameters' scope, and luckily x has already been initialized, so the assignment to y works fine.

However, the z in z + 1 finds z as a not-yet-initialized-at-that-moment parameter variable, so it never tries to find the z from the outer scope.

As we mentioned in "let Declarations" on page 8 earlier in this chapter, ES6 has a TDZ, which prevents a variable from being accessed in its uninitialized state. As such, the z + 1 default value expression throws a TDZ ReferenceError error.

Though it's not necessarily a good idea for code clarity, a default value expression can even be an inline function expression call—

commonly referred to as an immediately invoked function expression (IIFE):

```
function foo( x =
    (function(v){ return v + 11; })( 31 )
) {
    console.log( x );
}

foo();          // 42
```

There will very rarely be any cases where an IIFE (or any other executed inline function expression) will be appropriate for default value expressions. If you find yourself tempted to do this, take a step back and reevaluate!

 If the IIFE had tried to access the x identifier and had not declared its own x, this would also have been a TDZ error, just as discussed before.

The default value expression in the previous snippet is an IIFE in that in the sense that it's a function that's executed right inline, via (31). If we had left that part off, the default value assigned to x would have just been a function reference itself, perhaps like a default callback. There will probably be cases where that pattern will be quite useful, such as:

```
function ajax(url, cb = function(){}) {
    // ..
}

ajax( "http://some.url.1" );
```

In this case, we essentially want to default cb to be a no-op empty function call if not otherwise specified. The function expression is just a function reference, not a function call itself (no invoking () on the end of it), which accomplishes that goal.

Since the early days of JS, there's been a little-known but useful quirk available to us: Function.prototype is itself an empty no-op function. So, the declaration could have been cb = Function.prototype and saved the inline function expression creation.

Destructuring

ES6 introduces a new syntactic feature called *destructuring*, which may be a little less confusing if you instead think of it as a *structured assignment*. To understand this meaning, consider:

```
function foo() {
    return [1,2,3];
}

var tmp = foo(),
    a = tmp[0], b = tmp[1], c = tmp[2];

console.log( a, b, c );          // 1 2 3
```

As you can see, we created a manual assignment of the values in the array that foo() returns to individual variables a, b, and c, and to do so we (unfortunately) needed the tmp variable.

Similarly, we can do the following with objects:

```
function bar() {
    return {
        x: 4,
        y: 5,
        z: 6
    };
}

var tmp = bar(),
    x = tmp.x, y = tmp.y, z = tmp.z;

console.log( x, y, z );          // 4 5 6
```

The tmp.x property value is assigned to the x variable, and likewise for tmp.y to y and tmp.z to z.

Manually assigning indexed values from an array or properties from an object can be thought of as *structured assignment*. ES6 adds a dedicated syntax for *destructuring*, specifically *array destructuring* and *object destructuring*. This syntax eliminates the need for the tmp variable in the previous snippets, making them much cleaner. Consider:

```
var [ a, b, c ] = foo();
var { x: x, y: y, z: z } = bar();

console.log( a, b, c );          // 1 2 3
console.log( x, y, z );          // 4 5 6
```

You're likely more accustomed to seeing syntax like [a,b,c] on the righthand side of an = assignment, as the value being assigned.

Destructuring symmetrically flips that pattern, so that [a,b,c] on the lefthand side of the = assignment is treated as a kind of "pattern" for decomposing the righthand side array value into separate variable assignments.

Similarly, { x: x, y: y, z: z } specifies a "pattern" to decompose the object value from bar() into separate variable assignments.

Object Property Assignment Pattern

Let's dig into that { x: x, .. } syntax from the previous snippet. If the property name being matched is the same as the variable you want to declare, you can actually shorten the syntax:

```
var { x, y, z } = bar();

console.log( x, y, z );          // 4 5 6
```

Pretty cool, right?

But is { x, .. } leaving off the x: part or leaving off the : x part? We're actually leaving off the x: part when we use the shorter syntax. That may not seem like an important detail, but you'll understand its importance in just a moment.

If you can write the shorter form, why would you ever write out the longer form? Because that longer form actually allows you to assign a property to a different variable name, which can sometimes be quite useful:

```
var { x: bam, y: baz, z: bap } = bar();

console.log( bam, baz, bap );    // 4 5 6
console.log( x, y, z );          // ReferenceError
```

There's a subtle but super-important quirk to understand about this variation of the object destructuring form. To illustrate why it can be a gotcha you need to be careful of, let's consider the "pattern" of how normal object literals are specified:

```
var X = 10, Y = 20;

var o = { a: X, b: Y };

console.log( o.a, o.b );         // 10 20
```

In { a: X, b: Y }, we know that a is the object property, and X is the source value that gets assigned to it. In other words, the syntactic pattern is target: source, or more obviously, property-alias: value. We intuitively understand this because it's the same as = assignment, where the pattern is target = source.

However, when you use object destructuring assignment—that is, putting the { .. } object literal-looking syntax on the lefthand side of the = operator—you invert that target: source pattern.

Recall:

```
var { x: bam, y: baz, z: bap } = bar();
```

The syntactic pattern here is source: target (or value: variable-alias). x: bam means the x property is the source value and bam is the target variable to assign to. In other words, object literals are target <-- source, and object destructuring assignments are source --> target. See how that's flipped?

There's another way to think about this syntax though, which may help ease the confusion. Consider:

```
var aa = 10, bb = 20;

var o = { x: aa, y: bb };
var     { x: AA, y: BB } = o;

console.log( AA, BB );          // 10 20
```

In the { x: aa, y: bb } line, the x and y represent the object properties. In the { x: AA, y: BB } line, the x and y *also* represent the object properties.

Recall how earlier I asserted that { x, .. } was leaving off the x: part? In those two lines, if you erase the x: and y: parts in that snippet, you're left only with aa, bb and AA, BB, which in effect—only conceptually, not actually—are assignments from aa to AA and from bb to BB.

So, that symmetry may help to explain why the syntactic pattern was intentionally flipped for this ES6 feature.

I would have preferred the syntax to be `{ AA: x , BB: y }` for the destructuring assignment, as that would have preserved consistency of the more familiar `target: source` pattern for both usages. Alas, I'm having to train my brain for the inversion, as some readers may also have to do.

Not Just Declarations

So far, we've used destructuring assignment with `var` declarations (of course, they could also use `let` and `const`), but destructuring is a general assignment operation, not just a declaration.

Consider:

```
var a, b, c, x, y, z;

[a,b,c] = foo();
( { x, y, z } = bar() );

console.log( a, b, c );        // 1 2 3
console.log( x, y, z );        // 4 5 6
```

The variables can already be declared, and then the destructuring only does assignments, exactly as we've already seen.

For the object destructuring form specifically, when leaving off a `var`/`let`/`const` declarator, we had to surround the whole assignment expression in ( ), because otherwise the `{ .. }` on the lefthand side as the first element in the statement is taken to be a block statement instead of an object.

In fact, the assignment expressions (a, y, etc.) don't actually need to be just variable identifiers. Anything that's a valid assignment expression is allowed. For example:

```
var o = {};

[o.a, o.b, o.c] = foo();
( { x: o.x, y: o.y, z: o.z } = bar() );

console.log( o.a, o.b, o.c );        // 1 2 3
console.log( o.x, o.y, o.z );        // 4 5 6
```

You can even use computed property expressions in the destructuring. Consider:

```
var which = "x",
    o = {};

( { [which]: o[which] } = bar() );

console.log( o.x );                    // 4
```

The [which]: part is the computed property, which results in x—the property to destructure from the object in question as the source of the assignment. The o[which] part is just a normal object key reference, which equates to o.x as the target of the assignment.

You can use the general assignments to create object mappings/transformations, such as:

```
var o1 = { a: 1, b: 2, c: 3 },
    o2 = {};

( { a: o2.x, b: o2.y, c: o2.z } = o1 );

console.log( o2.x, o2.y, o2.z );    // 1 2 3
```

Or you can map an object to an array, such as:

```
var o1 = { a: 1, b: 2, c: 3 },
    a2 = [];

( { a: a2[0], b: a2[1], c: a2[2] } = o1 );

console.log( a2 );                     // [1,2,3]
```

Or the other way around:

```
var a1 = [ 1, 2, 3 ],
    o2 = {};

[ o2.a, o2.b, o2.c ] = a1;

console.log( o2.a, o2.b, o2.c );    // 1 2 3
```

Or you could reorder one array to another:

```
var a1 = [ 1, 2, 3 ],
    a2 = [];

[ a2[2], a2[0], a2[1] ] = a1;

console.log( a2 );                     // [2,3,1]
```

You can even solve the traditional "swap two variables" task without a temporary variable:

```
var x = 10, y = 20;

[ y, x ] = [ x, y ];

console.log( x, y );                 // 20 10
```

 Be careful: you shouldn't mix in declaration with assignment unless you want all of the assignment expressions *also* to be treated as declarations. Otherwise, you'll get syntax errors. That's why in the earlier example I had to do var a2 = [] separately from the [a2[0], ..] = .. destructuring assignment. It wouldn't make any sense to try var [a2[0], ..] = .., because a2[0] isn't a valid declaration identifier; it also obviously couldn't implicitly create a var a2 = [] declaration.

Repeated Assignments

The object destructuring form allows a source property (holding any value type) to be listed multiple times. For example:

```
var { a: X, a: Y } = { a: 1 };

X;  // 1
Y;  // 1
```

That also means you can both destructure a sub-object/array property and also capture the sub-object/array's value itself. Consider:

```
var { a: { x: X, x: Y }, a } = { a: { x: 1 } };

X;  // 1
Y;  // 1
a;  // { x: 1 }

( { a: X, a: Y, a: [ Z ] } = { a: [ 1 ] } );

X.push( 2 );
Y[0] = 10;

X;  // [10,2]
Y;  // [10,2]
Z;  // 1
```

A word of caution about destructuring: it may be tempting to list destructuring assignments all on a single line as has been done thus far in our discussion. However, it's a much better idea to spread destructuring assignment patterns over multiple lines, using proper indentation—much like you would in JSON or with an object literal value—for readability's sake.

```
// harder to read:
var { a: { b: [ c, d ], e: { f } }, g } = obj;

// better:
var {
    a: {
        b: [ c, d ],
        e: { f }
    },
    g
} = obj;
```

Remember: the purpose of destructuring is not just less typing, but more declarative readability.

Destructuring Assignment Expressions

The assignment expression with object or array destructuring has as its completion value the full righthand object/array value. Consider:

```
var o = { a:1, b:2, c:3 },
    a, b, c, p;

p = { a, b, c } = o;

console.log( a, b, c );      // 1 2 3
p === o;                     // true
```

In the previous snippet, p was assigned the o object reference, not one of the a, b, or c values. The same is true of array destructuring:

```
var o = [1,2,3],
    a, b, c, p;

p = { a, b, c } = o;

console.log( a, b, c );      // 1 2 3
p === o;                     // true
```

By carrying the object/array value through as the completion, you can chain destructuring assignment expressions together:

```
var o = { a:1, b:2, c:3 },
    p = [4,5,6],
```

```
    a, b, c, x, y, z;

( {a} = {b,c} = o );
[x,y] = [z] = p;

console.log( a, b, c );          // 1 2 3
console.log( x, y, z );          // 4 5 4
```

Too Many, Too Few, Just Enough

With both array destructuring assignment and object destructuring assignment, you do not have to assign all the values that are present. For example:

```
var [,b] = foo();
var { x, z } = bar();

console.log( b, x, z );          // 2 4 6
```

The 1 and 3 values that came back from foo() are discarded, as is the 5 value from bar().

Similarly, if you try to assign more values than are present in the value you're destructuring/decomposing, you get graceful fallback to undefined, as you'd expect:

```
var [,,c,d] = foo();
var { w, z } = bar();

console.log( c, z );             // 3 6
console.log( d, w );             // undefined undefined
```

This behavior follows symmetrically from the earlier stated "unde fined is missing" principle.

We examined the ... operator earlier in this chapter, and saw that it can sometimes be used to spread an array value out into its separate values, and sometimes it can be used to do the opposite: to gather a set of values together into an array.

In addition to the gather/rest usage in function declarations, ... can perform the same behavior in destructuring assignments. To illustrate, let's recall a snippet from earlier in this chapter:

```
var a = [2,3,4];
var b = [ 1, ...a, 5 ];

console.log( b );                // [1,2,3,4,5]
```

Here we see that ...a is spreading a out, because it appears in the array [..] value position. If ...a appears in an array destructuring position, it performs the gather behavior:

```
var a = [2,3,4];
var [ b, ...c ] = a;

console.log( b, c );                    // 2 [3,4]
```

The var [..] = a destructuring assignment spreads a out to be assigned to the pattern described inside the [..]. The first part names b for the first value in a (2). But then ...c gathers the rest of the values (3 and 4) into an array and calls it c.

 We've seen how ... works with arrays, but what about with objects? It's not an ES6 feature, but see Chapter 8 for discussion of a possible "beyond ES6" feature where ... works with spreading or gathering objects.

Default Value Assignment

Both forms of destructuring can offer a default value option for an assignment, using the = syntax similar to the default function argument values discussed earlier.

Consider:

```
var [ a = 3, b = 6, c = 9, d = 12 ] = foo();
var { x = 5, y = 10, z = 15, w = 20 } = bar();

console.log( a, b, c, d );       // 1 2 3 12
console.log( x, y, z, w );       // 4 5 6 20
```

You can combine the default value assignment with the alternative assignment expression syntax covered earlier. For example:

```
var { x, y, z, w: WW = 20 } = bar();

console.log( x, y, z, WW );      // 4 5 6 20
```

Be careful about confusing yourself (or other developers who read your code) if you use an object or array as the default value in a destructuring. You can create some really hard-to-understand code:

```
var x = 200, y = 300, z = 100;
var o1 = { x: { y: 42 }, z: { y: z } };
```

```
( { y: x = { y: y } } = o1 );
( { z: y = { y: z } } = o1 );
( { x: z = { y: x } } = o1 );
```

Can you tell from that snippet what values x, y, and z have at the end? Takes a moment of pondering, I would imagine. I'll end the suspense:

```
console.log( x.y, y.y, z.y );        // 300 100 42
```

The takeaway here: destructuring is great and can be very useful, but it's also a sharp sword that can cause injury (to someone's brain) if used unwisely.

Nested Destructuring

If the values you're destructuring have nested objects or arrays, you can destructure those nested values as well:

```
var a1 = [ 1, [2, 3, 4], 5 ];
var o1 = { x: { y: { z: 6 } } };

var [ a, [ b, c, d ], e ] = a1;
var { x: { y: { z: w } } } = o1;

console.log( a, b, c, d, e );        // 1 2 3 4 5
console.log( w );                     // 6
```

Nested destructuring can be a simple way to flatten out object namespaces. For example:

```
var App = {
    model: {
        User: function(){ .. }
    }
};

// instead of:
// var User = App.model.User;

var { model: { User } } = App;
```

Destructuring Parameters

In the following snippet, can you spot the assignment?

```
function foo(x) {
    console.log( x );
}

foo( 42 );
```

The assignment is kinda hidden: 42 (the argument) is assigned to x (the parameter) when foo(42) is executed. If parameter/argument pairing is an assignment, then it stands to reason that it's an assignment that could be destructured, right? Of course!

Consider array destructuring for parameters:

```
function foo( [ x, y ] ) {
    console.log( x, y );
}
```

```
foo( [ 1, 2 ] );            // 1 2
foo( [ 1 ] );               // 1 undefined
foo( [] );                  // undefined undefined
```

Object destructuring for parameters works, too:

```
function foo( { x, y } ) {
    console.log( x, y );
}
```

```
foo( { y: 1, x: 2 } );      // 2 1
foo( { y: 42 } );           // undefined 42
foo( {} );                  // undefined undefined
```

This technique is an approximation of named arguments (a long requested feature for JS!), in that the properties on the object map to the destructured parameters of the same names. That also means that we get optional parameters (in any position) for free; as you can see, leaving off the x "parameter" worked as we'd expect.

Of course, all the previously discussed variations of destructuring are available to us with parameter destructuring, including nested destructuring, default values, and more. Destructuring also mixes fine with other ES6 function parameter capabilities, like default parameter values and rest/gather parameters.

Consider these quick illustrations (certainly not exhaustive of the possible variations):

```
function f1([ x=2, y=3, z ]) { .. }
function f2([ x, y, ...z], w) { .. }
function f3([ x, y, ...z], ...w) { .. }

function f4({ x: X, y }) { .. }
function f5({ x: X = 10, y = 20 }) { .. }
function f6({ x = 10 } = {}, { y } = { y: 10 }) { .. }
```

Let's take one example from this snippet and examine it, for illustration purposes:

```
function f3([ x, y, ...z], ...w) {
    console.log( x, y, z, w );
}

f3( [] );                          // undefined undefined [] []
f3( [1,2,3,4], 5, 6 );            // 1 2 [3,4] [5,6]
```

There are two ... operators in use here, and they're both gathering values in arrays (z and w), though ...z gathers from the rest of the values left over in the first array argument, while ...w gathers from the rest of the main arguments left over after the first.

Destructuring Defaults + Parameter Defaults

There's one subtle point you should be particularly careful to notice —the difference in behavior between a destructuring default value and a function parameter default value. For example:

```
function f6({ x = 10 } = {}, { y } = { y: 10 }) {
    console.log( x, y );
}

f6();                              // 10 10
```

At first, it would seem that we've declared a default value of 10 for both the x and y parameters, but in two different ways. However, these two different approaches will behave differently in certain cases, and the difference is awfully subtle.

Consider:

```
f6( {}, {} );                      // 10 undefined
```

Wait, why did that happen? It's pretty clear that named parameter x is defaulting to 10 if not passed as a property of that same name in the first argument's object.

But what about y being undefined? The { y: 10 } value is an object as a function parameter default value, not a destructuring default value. As such, it only applies if the second argument is not passed at all, or is passed as undefined.

In the previous snippet, we *are* passing a second argument ({}), so the default { y: 10 } value is not used, and the { y } destructuring occurs against the passed-in {} empty object value.

Now, compare { y } = { y: 10 } to { x = 10 } = {}.

For the x's form usage, if the first function argument is omitted or undefined, the {} empty object default applies. Then, whatever value is in the first argument position—either the default {} or whatever you passed in—is destructured with the { x = 10 }, which checks to see if an x property is found, and if not found (or undefined), the 10 default value is applied to the x named parameter.

Deep breath. Read back over those last few paragraphs a couple of times. Let's review via code:

```
function f6({ x = 10 } = {}, { y } = { y: 10 }) {
    console.log( x, y );
}

f6();                        // 10 10
f6( undefined, undefined );  // 10 10
f6( {}, undefined );         // 10 10

f6( {}, {} );                // 10 undefined
f6( undefined, {} );         // 10 undefined

f6( { x: 2 }, { y: 3 } );    // 2 3
```

It would generally seem that the defaulting behavior of the x parameter is probably the more desirable and sensible case compared to that of y. As such, it's important to understand why and how { x = 10 } = {} form is different from { y } = { y: 10 } form.

If that's still a bit fuzzy, go back and read it again, and play with this yourself. Your future self will thank you for taking the time to get this very subtle gotcha nuance detail straight.

Nested Defaults: Destructured and Restructured

Although it may at first be difficult to grasp, an interesting idiom emerges for setting defaults for a nested object's properties: using object destructuring along with what I'd call *restructuring*.

Consider a set of defaults in a nested object structure, like the following:

```
// taken from:
// http://es-discourse.com/t/partial-default-arguments/120/7

var defaults = {
    options: {
        remove: true,
```

```
            enable: false,
            instance: {}
        },
        log: {
            warn: true,
            error: true
        }
    };
```

Now, let's say you have an object called `config`, which has some of these applied, but perhaps not all, and you'd like to set all the defaults into this object in the missing spots, but not override specific settings already present:

```
    var config = {
        options: {
            remove: false,
            instance: null
        }
    };
```

You can of course do so manually, as you might have done in the past:

```
    config.options = config.options || {};
    config.options.remove = (config.options.remove !== undefined) ?
        config.options.remove : defaults.options.remove;
    config.options.enable = (config.options.enable !== undefined) ?
        config.options.enable : defaults.options.enable;
    ...
```

Yuck.

Others may prefer the assign-overwrite approach to this task. You might be tempted by the ES6 `Object.assign(..)` utility (see Chapter 6) to clone the properties first from `defaults` and then overwritten with the cloned properties from `config`, as so:

```
    config = Object.assign( {}, defaults, config );
```

That looks way nicer, huh? But there's a major problem! `Object.assign(..)` is shallow, which means when it copies `defaults.options`, it just copies that object reference, not deep cloning that object's properties to a `config.options` object. `Object.assign(..)` would need to be applied (sort of "recursively") at all levels of your object's tree to get the deep cloning you're expecting.

Many JS utility libraries/frameworks provide their own option for deep cloning of an object, but those approaches and their gotchas are beyond our scope to discuss here.

So let's examine if ES6 object destructuring with defaults can help at all:

```
config.options = config.options || {};
config.log = config.log || {};
{
    options: {
        remove: config.options.remove = default.options.remove,
        enable: config.options.enable = default.options.enable,
        instance: config.options.instance =
                    default.options.instance
    } = {},
    log: {
        warn: config.log.warn = default.log.warn,
        error: config.log.error = default.log.error
    } = {}
} = config;
```

Not as nice as the false promise of `Object.assign(..)` (being that it's shallow only), but it's better than the manual approach by a fair bit, I think. It is still unfortunately verbose and repetitive, though.

The previous snippet's approach works because I'm hacking the destructuring and defaults mechanism to do the property `===` unde fined checks and assignment decisions for me. It's a trick in that I'm destructuring `config` (see the `= config` at the end of the snippet), but I'm reassigning all the destructured values right back into `config`, with the `config.options.enable` assignment references.

Still too much, though. Let's see if we can make anything better.

The following trick works best if you know that all the various properties you're destructuring are uniquely named. You can still do it even if that's not the case, but it's not as nice—you'll have to do the destructuring in stages, or create unique local variables as temporary aliases.

If we fully destructure all the properties into top-level variables, we can then immediately restructure to reconstitute the original nested object structure.

But all those temporary variables hanging around would pollute scope. So, let's use block scoping (see "Block-Scoped Declarations" on page 7 earlier in this chapter) with a general { } enclosing block:

```
// merge `defaults` into `config`
{
    // destructure (with default value assignments)
    let {
        options: {
            remove = defaults.options.remove,
            enable = defaults.options.enable,
            instance = defaults.options.instance
        } = {},
        log: {
            warn = defaults.log.warn,
            error = defaults.log.error
        } = {}
    } = config;

    // restructure
    config = {
        options: { remove, enable, instance },
        log: { warn, error }
    };
}
```

That seems a fair bit nicer, huh?

 You could also accomplish the scope enclosure with an arrow IIFE instead of the general { } block and let declarations. Your destructuring assignments/defaults would be in the parameter list and your restructuring would be the return statement in the function body.

The { warn, error } syntax in the restructuring part may look new to you; that's called "concise properties" and we cover it in the next section!

Object Literal Extensions

ES6 adds a number of important convenience extensions to the humble { .. } object literal.

Concise Properties

You're certainly familiar with declaring object literals in this form:

```
var x = 2, y = 3,
    o = {
        x: x,
        y: y
    };
```

If it's always felt redundant to say x: x all over, there's good news. If you need to define a property that is the same name as a lexical identifier, you can shorten it from x: x to x. Consider:

```
var x = 2, y = 3,
    o = {
        x,
        y
    };
```

Concise Methods

In a similar spirit to concise properties we just examined, functions attached to properties in object literals also have a concise form, for convenience.

The old way:

```
var o = {
    x: function(){
        // ..
    },
    y: function(){
        // ..
    }
}
```

And as of ES6:

```
var o = {
    x() {
        // ..
    },
    y() {
        // ..
    }
}
```

While x() { .. } seems to just be shorthand for x: function(){ .. }, concise methods have special behaviors that their older counterparts don't; specifically, the allowance for super (see "Object super" on page 47 later in this chapter).

Generators (see Chapter 4) also have a concise method form:

```
var o = {
    *foo() { .. }
};
```

Concisely Unnamed

While that convenience shorthand is quite attractive, there's a subtle gotcha to be aware of. To illustrate, let's examine pre-ES6 code like the following, which you might try to refactor to use concise methods:

```
function runSomething(o) {
    var x = Math.random(),
        y = Math.random();

    return o.something( x, y );
}

runSomething( {
    something: function something(x,y) {
        if (x > y) {
            // recursively call with `x`
            // and `y` swapped
            return something( y, x );
        }

        return y - x;
    }
} );
```

This obviously silly code just generates two random numbers and subtracts the smaller from the bigger. But what's important here isn't what it does, but rather how it's defined. Let's focus on the object literal and function definition, as we see here:

```
runSomething( {
    something: function something(x,y) {
        // ..
    }
} );
```

Why do we say both something: and function something? Isn't that redundant? Actually, no, both are needed for different purposes. The property something is how we can call o.something(..), sort of like its public name. But the second something is a lexical name to refer to the function from inside itself, for recursion purposes.

Can you see why the line `return something(y,x)` needs the name `something` to refer to the function? There's no lexical name for the object, such that it could have said `return o.something(y,x)` or something of that sort.

That's actually a pretty common practice when the object literal does have an identifying name, such as:

```
var controller = {
    makeRequest: function(..){
        // ..
        controller.makeRequest(..);
    }
};
```

Is this a good idea? Perhaps, perhaps not. You're assuming that the name `controller` will always point to the object in question. But it very well may not—the `makeRequest(..)` function doesn't control the outer code and so can't force that to be the case. This could come back to bite you.

Others prefer to use `this` to define such things:

```
var controller = {
    makeRequest: function(..){
        // ..
        this.makeRequest(..);
    }
};
```

That looks fine, and should work if you always invoke the method as `controller.makeRequest(..)`. But you now have a `this` binding gotcha if you do something like:

```
btn.addEventListener( "click", controller.makeRequest, false );
```

Of course, you can solve that by passing `controller.makeRe quest.bind(controller)` as the handler reference to bind the event to. But yuck—it isn't very appealing.

Or what if your inner `this.makeRequest(..)` call needs to be made from a nested function? You'll have another `this` binding hazard, which people will often solve with the hacky `var self = this`, such as:

```
var controller = {
    makeRequest: function(..){
        var self = this;
```

```
    btn.addEventListener( "click", function(){
        // ..
        self.makeRequest(..);
    }, false );
    }
};
```

More yuck.

 For more information on this binding rules and gotchas, see Chapters 1–2 of the *this & Object Prototypes* title of this series.

OK, what does all this have to do with concise methods? Recall our something(..) method definition:

```
runSomething( {
    something: function something(x,y) {
        // ..
    }
} );
```

The second something here provides a super convenient lexical identifier that will always point to the function itself, giving us the perfect reference for recursion, event binding/unbinding, and so on —no messing around with this or trying to use an untrustable object reference.

Great!

So, now we try to refactor that function reference to this ES6 concise method form:

```
runSomething( {
    something(x,y) {
        if (x > y) {
            return something( y, x );
        }

        return y - x;
    }
} );
```

Seems fine at first glance, except this code will break. The return something(..) call will not find a something identifier, so you'll get a ReferenceError. Oops. But why?

The above ES6 snippet is interpreted as meaning:

```
runSomething( {
    something: function(x,y){
        if (x > y) {
            return something( y, x );
        }

        return y - x;
    }
} );
```

Look closely. Do you see the problem? The concise method definition implies something: function(x,y). See how the second some thing we were relying on has been omitted? In other words, concise methods imply anonymous function expressions.

Yeah, yuck.

 You may be tempted to think that => arrow functions are a good solution here, but they're equally insufficient, as they're also anonymous function expressions. We'll cover them in "Arrow Functions" on page 54 later in this chapter.

The partially redeeming news is that our something(x,y) concise method won't be totally anonymous. See "Function Names" on page 200 in Chapter 7 for information about ES6 function name inference rules. That won't help us for our recursion, but it helps with debugging at least.

So what are we left to conclude about concise methods? They're short and sweet, and a nice convenience. But you should only use them if you're never going to need them to do recursion or event binding/unbinding. Otherwise, stick to your old-school something: function something(..) method definitions.

A lot of your methods are probably going to benefit from concise method definitions, so that's great news! Just be careful of the few where there's an un-naming hazard.

ES5 Getter/Setter

Technically, ES5 defined getter/setter literals forms, but they didn't seem to get used much, mostly due to the lack of transpilers to handle that new syntax (the only major new syntax added in ES5, really). So while it's not a new ES6 feature, we'll briefly refresh on that form, as it's probably going to be much more useful with ES6 going forward.

Consider:

```
var o = {
    __id: 10,
    get id() { return this.__id++; },
    set id(v) { this.__id = v; }
}

o.id;           // 10
o.id;           // 11
o.id = 20;
o.id;           // 20

// and:
o.__id;         // 21
o.__id;         // 21--still!
```

These getter and setter literal forms are also present in classes; see Chapter 3.

 It may not be obvious, but the setter literal must have exactly one declared parameter; omitting it or listing others is illegal syntax. The single required parameter *can* use destructuring and defaults (e.g., set id({ id: v = 0 }) { .. }), but the gather/rest ... is not allowed (set id(...v) { .. }).

Computed Property Names

You've probably been in a situation like the following snippet, where you have one or more property names that come from some sort of expression and thus can't be put into the object literal:

```
var prefix = "user_";

var o = {
    baz: function(..){ .. }
};

o[ prefix + "foo" ] = function(..){ .. };
o[ prefix + "bar" ] = function(..){ .. };
..
```

ES6 adds a syntax to the object literal definition that allows you to specify an expression that should be computed, whose result is the property name assigned. Consider:

```
var prefix = "user_";

var o = {
    baz: function(..){ .. },
    [ prefix + "foo" ]: function(..){ .. },
    [ prefix + "bar" ]: function(..){ .. }
    ..
};
```

Any valid expression can appear inside the [..] that sits in the property name position of the object literal definition.

Probably the most common use of computed property names will be with Symbols (which we cover in "Symbols" on page 80 later in this chapter), such as:

```
var o = {
    [Symbol.toStringTag]: "really cool thing",
    ..
};
```

Symbol.toStringTag is a special built-in value, which we evaluate with the [..] syntax, so we can assign the "really cool thing" value to the special property name.

Computed property names can also appear as the name of a concise method or a concise generator:

```
var o = {
    ["f" + "oo"]() { .. }    // computed concise method
    *["b" + "ar"]() { .. }   // computed concise generator
};
```

Setting [[Prototype]]

We won't cover prototypes in detail here, so for more information, see the *this & Object Prototypes* title of this series.

Sometimes it will be helpful to assign the [[Prototype]] of an object at the same time you're declaring its object literal. The following has been a nonstandard extension in many JS engines for a while, but is standardized as of ES6:

```
var o1 = {
    // ..
};
```

```
var o2 = {
    __proto__: o1,
    // ..
};
```

o2 is declared with a normal object literal, but it's also [[Prototype]]-linked to o1. The __proto__ property name here can also be a string "__proto__", but note that it *cannot* be the result of a computed property name (see the previous section).

__proto__ is controversial, to say the least. It's a decades-old proprietary extension to JS that is finally standardized, somewhat begrudgingly it seems, in ES6. Many developers feel it shouldn't ever be used. In fact, it's in "Annex B" of ES6, which is the section that lists things JS feels it has to standardize for compatibility reasons only.

Though I'm narrowly endorsing __proto__ as a key in an object literal definition, I definitely do not endorse using it in its object property form, like o.__proto__. That form is both a getter and setter (again for compatibility reasons), but there are definitely better options. See the *this & Object Prototypes* title of this series for more information.

For setting the [[Prototype]] of an existing object, you can use the ES6 utility Object.setPrototypeOf(..). Consider:

```
var o1 = {
    // ..
};

var o2 = {
    // ..
};

Object.setPrototypeOf( o2, o1 );
```

We'll discuss Object again in Chapter 6. "Object.setPrototypeOf(..) Static Function" provides additional details on Object.setPrototypeOf(..). Also see "Object.assign(..) Static Function" on page 188 for another form that relates o2 prototypically to o1.

Object super

super is typically thought of as being only related to classes. However, due to JS's classless-objects-with-prototypes nature, super is equally effective, and nearly the same in behavior, with plain objects' concise methods.

Consider:

```
var o1 = {
    foo() {
        console.log( "o1:foo" );
    }
};

var o2 = {
    foo() {
        super.foo();
        console.log( "o2:foo" );
    }
};

Object.setPrototypeOf( o2, o1 );

o2.foo();        // o1:foo
                 // o2:foo
```

 super is only allowed in concise methods, not regular function expression properties. It also is only allowed in super.XXX form (for property/method access), not in super() form.

The super reference in the o2.foo() method is locked statically to o2, and specifically to the [[Prototype]] of o2. super here would basically be Object.getPrototypeOf(o2)—resolves to o1 of course —which is how it finds and calls o1.foo().

For complete details on super, see "Classes" on page 135 in Chapter 3.

Template Literals

At the very outset of this section, I'm going to have to call out the name of this ES6 feature as being awfully... misleading, depending on your experiences with what the word *template* means.

Many developers think of templates as being reusable renderable pieces of text, such as the capability provided by most template engines (Mustache, Handlebars, etc.). ES6's use of the word *template* would imply something similar, like a way to declare inline template literals that can be re-rendered. However, that's not at all the right way to think about this feature.

So, before we go on, I'm renaming it to what it should have been called: *interpolated string literals* (or *interpoliterals* for short).

You're already well aware of declaring string literals with " or ' delimiters, and you also know that these are not *smart strings* (as some languages have), where the contents would be parsed for interpolation expressions.

However, ES6 introduces a new type of string literal, using the ` backtick as the delimiter. These string literals allow basic string interpolation expressions to be embedded, which are then automatically parsed and evaluated.

Here's the old pre-ES6 way:

```
var name = "Kyle";

var greeting = "Hello " + name + "!";

console.log( greeting );          // "Hello Kyle!"
console.log( typeof greeting );   // "string"
```

Now, consider the new ES6 way:

```
var name = "Kyle";

var greeting = `Hello ${name}!`;

console.log( greeting );          // "Hello Kyle!"
console.log( typeof greeting );   // "string"
```

As you can see, we used the `..` around a series of characters, which are interpreted as a string literal, but any expressions of the form ${..} are parsed and evaluated inline immediately. The fancy term for such parsing and evaluating is *interpolation* (much more accurate than templating).

The result of the interpolated string literal expression is just a plain old normal string, assigned to the greeting variable.

`typeof greeting == "string"` illustrates why it's important not to think of these entities as special template values, as you cannot assign the unevaluated form of the literal to something and reuse it. The `` `..` `` string literal is more like an IIFE in the sense that it's automatically evaluated inline. The result of a `` `..` `` string literal is, simply, just a string.

One really nice benefit of interpolated string literals is they are allowed to split across multiple lines:

```
var text =
`Now is the time for all good men
to come to the aid of their
country!`;

console.log( text );
// Now is the time for all good men
// to come to the aid of their
// country!
```

The line breaks (newlines) in the interpolated string literal were preserved in the string value.

Unless appearing as explicit escape sequences in the literal value, the value of the \r carriage return character (code point U+000D) or the value of the \r\n carriage return + line feed sequence (code points U+000D and U+000A) are both normalized to a \n line feed character (code point U+000A). Don't worry though; this normalization is rare and would likely only happen if copy-pasting text into your JS file.

Interpolated Expressions

Any valid expression is allowed to appear inside ${..} in an interpolated string literal, including function calls, inline function expression calls, and even other interpolated string literals!

Consider:

```
function upper(s) {
    return s.toUpperCase();
}

var who = "reader";

var text =
`A very ${upper( "warm" )} welcome
```

```
to all of you ${upper( `${who}s` )}!`;

console.log( text );
// A very WARM welcome
// to all of you READERS!
```

Here, the inner `` `${who}s` `` interpolated string literal was a little bit nicer convenience for us when combining the who variable with the "s" string, as opposed to who + "s". There will be cases where nesting interpolated string literals is helpful, but be wary if you find yourself doing that kind of thing often, or if you find yourself nesting several levels deep.

If that's the case, the odds are good that your string value production could benefit from some abstractions.

 As a word of caution, be very careful about the readability of your code with such newfound power. Just like with default value expressions and destructuring assignment expressions, just because you *can* do something doesn't mean you *should* do it. Never go so overboard with new ES6 tricks that your code becomes more clever than you or your other team members.

Expression Scope

One quick note about the scope that is used to resolve variables in expressions. I mentioned earlier that an interpolated string literal is kind of like an IIFE, and it turns out thinking about it like that explains the scoping behavior as well.

Consider:

```
function foo(str) {
    var name = "foo";
    console.log( str );
}

function bar() {
    var name = "bar";
    foo( `Hello from ${name}!` );
}

var name = "global";

bar();                      // "Hello from bar!"
```

At the moment the `..` string literal is expressed, inside the bar() function, the scope available to it finds bar()'s name variable with value "bar". Neither the global name nor foo(..)'s name matter. In other words, an interpolated string literal is just lexically scoped where it appears, not dynamically scoped in any way.

Tagged Template Literals

Again, renaming the feature for sanity sake: *tagged string literals*.

To be honest, this is one of the cooler tricks that ES6 offers. It may seem a little strange, and perhaps not all that generally practical at first. But once you've spent some time with it, tagged string literals may just surprise you in their usefulness.

For example:

```
function foo(strings, ...values) {
    console.log( strings );
    console.log( values );
}

var desc = "awesome";

foo`Everything is ${desc}!`;
// [ "Everything is ", "!"]
// [ "awesome" ]
```

Let's take a moment to consider what's happening in the previous snippet. First, the most jarring thing that jumps out is foo`Every thing...`;. That doesn't look like anything we've seen before. What is it?

It's essentially a special kind of function call that doesn't need the (..). The *tag*—the foo part before the `..` string literal—is a function value that should be called. Actually, it can be any expression that results in a function, even a function call that returns another function, like:

```
function bar() {
    return function foo(strings, ...values) {
        console.log( strings );
        console.log( values );
    }
}

var desc = "awesome";
```

```
bar()`Everything is ${desc}!`;
// [ "Everything is ", "!"]
// [ "awesome" ]
```

But what gets passed to the `foo(..)` function when invoked as a tag for a string literal?

The first argument—we called it `strings`—is an array of all the plain strings (the stuff between any interpolated expressions). We get two values in the `strings` array: `"Everything is "` and `"!"`.

For convenience sake in our example, we then gather up all subsequent arguments into an array called `values` using the `...` gather/rest operator (see "Spread/Rest" on page 15 earlier in this chapter), though you could of course have left them as individually named parameters following the `strings` parameter.

The argument(s) gathered into our `values` array are the results of the already-evaluated interpolation expressions found in the string literal. So obviously the only element in `values` in our example is `"awesome"`.

You can think of these two arrays as: the values in `values` are the separators if you were to splice them in between the values in `strings`, and then if you joined everything together, you'd get the complete interpolated string value.

A tagged string literal is like a processing step after the interpolation expressions are evaluated but before the final string value is compiled, allowing you more control over generating the string from the literal.

Typically, the string literal tag function (`foo(..)` in the previous snippets) should compute an appropriate string value and return it, so that you can use the tagged string literal as a value just like untagged string literals:

```
function tag(strings, ...values) {
    return strings.reduce( function(s,v,idx){
        return s + (idx > 0 ? values[idx-1] : "") + v;
    }, "" );
}

var desc = "awesome";

var text = tag`Everything is ${desc}!`;

console.log( text );            // Everything is awesome!
```

In this snippet, `tag(..)` is a pass-through operation, in that it doesn't perform any special modifications, but just uses `reduce(..)` to loop over and splice/interleave `strings` and `values` together the same way an untagged string literal would have done.

So what are some practical uses? There are many advanced ones that are beyond our scope to discuss here. But here's a simple idea that formats numbers as U.S. dollars (sort of like basic localization):

```
function dollabillsyall(strings, ...values) {
    return strings.reduce( function(s,v,idx){
        if (idx > 0) {
            if (typeof values[idx-1] == "number") {
                // look, also using interpolated
                // string literals!
                s += `$${values[idx-1].toFixed( 2 )}`;
            }
            else {
                s += values[idx-1];
            }
        }

        return s + v;
    }, "" );
}

var amt1 = 11.99,
    amt2 = amt1 * 1.08,
    name = "Kyle";

var text = dollabillsyall
`Thanks for your purchase, ${name}! Your
product cost was ${amt1}, which with tax
comes out to ${amt2}.`

console.log( text );
// Thanks for your purchase, Kyle! Your
// product cost was $11.99, which with tax
// comes out to $12.95.
```

If a `number` value is encountered in the `values` array, we put "$" in front of it and format it to two decimal places with `toFixed(2)`. Otherwise, we let the value pass-through untouched.

Raw Strings

In the previous snippets, our tag functions receive the first argument we called `strings`, which is an array. But there's an additional bit of data included: the raw unprocessed versions of all the strings. You can access those raw string values using the `.raw` property, like this:

```
function showraw(strings, ...values) {
    console.log( strings );
    console.log( strings.raw );
}

showraw`Hello\nWorld`;
// [ "Hello
// World" ]
// [ "Hello\nWorld" ]
```

The raw version of the value preserves the raw escaped `\n` sequence (the `\` and the `n` are separate characters), while the processed version considers it a single newline character. However, the earlier mentioned line-ending normalization is applied to both values.

ES6 comes with a built-in function that can be used as a string literal tag: `String.raw(..)`. It simply passes through the raw versions of the `strings`:

```
console.log( `Hello\nWorld` );
// Hello
// World


console.log( String.raw`Hello\nWorld` );
// Hello\nWorld

String.raw`Hello\nWorld`.length;
// 12
```

Other uses for string literal tags include special processing for internationalization, localization, and more!

Arrow Functions

We've touched on `this` binding complications with functions earlier in this chapter, and they're covered at length in the *this & Object Prototypes* title of this series. It's important to understand the frustrations that `this`-based programming with normal functions brings, because that is the primary motivation for the new ES6 `=>` arrow function feature.

Let's first illustrate what an arrow function looks like, as compared to normal functions:

```
function foo(x,y) {
    return x + y;
}

// versus

var foo = (x,y) => x + y;
```

The arrow function definition consists of a parameter list (of zero or more parameters, and surrounding (..) if there's not exactly one parameter), followed by the => marker, followed by a function body.

So, in the previous snippet, the arrow function is just the (x,y) => x + y part, and that function reference happens to be assigned to the variable foo.

The body only needs to be enclosed by { .. } if there's more than one expression, or if the body consists of a non-expression statement. If there's only one expression, and you omit the surrounding { .. }, there's an implied return in front of the expression, as illustrated in the previous snippet.

Here's some other arrow function variations to consider:

```
var f1 = () => 12;
var f2 = x => x * 2;
var f3 = (x,y) => {
    var z = x * 2 + y;
    y++;
    x *= 3;
    return (x + y + z) / 2;
};
```

Arrow functions are *always* function expressions; there is no arrow function declaration. It also should be clear that they are anonymous function expressions—they have no named reference for the purposes of recursion or event binding/unbinding—though "Function Names" on page 200 in Chapter 7 will describe ES6's function name inference rules for debugging purposes.

 All the capabilities of normal function parameters are available to arrow functions, including default values, destructuring, rest parameters, and so on.

Arrow functions have a nice, shorter syntax, which makes them on the surface very attractive for writing terser code. Indeed, nearly all literature on ES6 (other than the titles in this series) seems to immediately and exclusively adopt the arrow function as "the new function."

It is telling that nearly all examples in our discussion of arrow functions are short single statement utilities, such as those passed as callbacks to various utilities. For example:

```
var a = [1,2,3,4,5];

a = a.map( v => v * 2 );

console.log( a );                // [2,4,6,8,10]
```

In those cases, where you have such inline function expressions, and they fit the pattern of computing a quick calculation in a single statement and returning that result, arrow functions indeed look to be an attractive and lightweight alternative to the more verbose func tion keyword and syntax.

Most people tend to *ooh and aah* at nice terse examples like that, as I imagine you just did!

However, I would caution you that it would seem to me somewhat a misapplication of this feature to use arrow function syntax with otherwise normal, multistatement functions, especially those that would otherwise be naturally expressed as function declarations.

Recall the dollabillsyall(..) string literal tag function from earlier in this chapter—let's change it to use => syntax:

```
var dollabillsyall = (strings, ...values) =>
    strings.reduce( (s,v,idx) => {
        if (idx > 0) {
            if (typeof values[idx-1] == "number") {
                // look, also using interpolated
                // string literals!
                s += `$${values[idx-1].toFixed( 2 )}`;
            }
            else {
                s += values[idx-1];
            }
        }

        return s + v;
    }, "" );
```

In this example, the only modifications I made were the removal of `function`, `return`, and some `{ .. }`, and then the insertion of `=>` and a `var`. Is this a significant improvement in the readability of the code? Meh.

I'd actually argue that the lack of `return` and outer `{ .. }` partially obscures the fact that the `reduce(..)` call is the only statement in the `dollabillsyall(..)` function and that its result is the intended result of the call. Also, the trained eye, which is so used to hunting for the word `function` in code to find scope boundaries, now needs to look for the `=>` marker, which can definitely be harder to find in the thick of the code.

While not a hard-and-fast rule, I'd say that the readability gains from `=>` arrow function conversion are inversely proportional to the length of the function being converted. The longer the function, the less `=>` helps; the shorter the function, the more `=>` can shine.

I think it's probably more sensible and reasonable to adopt `=>` for the places in code where you do need short inline function expressions, but leave your normal-length main functions as is.

Not Just Shorter Syntax, But this

Most of the popular attention toward `=>` has been on saving those precious keystrokes by dropping `function`, `return`, and `{ .. }` from your code.

But there's a big detail we've skipped over so far. I said at the beginning of the section that `=>` functions are closely related to `this` binding behavior. In fact, `=>` arrow functions are *primarily designed* to alter `this` behavior in a specific way, solving a particular and common pain point with `this`-aware coding.

The saving of keystrokes is a red herring, a misleading sideshow at best.

Let's revisit another example from earlier in this chapter:

```
var controller = {
    makeRequest: function(..){
        var self = this;

        btn.addEventListener( "click", function(){
            // ..
            self.makeRequest(..);
```

```
        }, false );
    }
};
```

We used the `var self = this` hack, and then referenced `self.mak eRequest(..)`, because inside the callback function we're passing to `addEventListener(..)`, the `this` binding will not be the same as it is in `makeRequest(..)` itself. In other words, because `this` bindings are dynamic, we fall back to the predictability of lexical scope via the `self` variable.

Herein we finally can see the primary design characteristic of `=>` arrow functions. Inside arrow functions, the `this` binding is not dynamic, but is instead lexical. In the previous snippet, if we used an arrow function for the callback, `this` will be predictably what we wanted it to be.

Consider:

```
var controller = {
    makeRequest: function(..){
        btn.addEventListener( "click", () => {
            // ..
            this.makeRequest(..);
        }, false );
    }
};
```

Lexical `this` in the arrow function callback in the previous snippet now points to the same value as in the enclosing `makeRequest(..)` function. In other words, `=>` is a syntactic stand-in for `var self = this`.

In cases where `var self = this` (or, alternatively, a function `.bind(this)` call) would normally be helpful, `=>` arrow functions are a nicer alternative operating on the same principle. Sounds great, right?

Not quite so simple.

If `=>` replaces `var self = this` or `.bind(this)` and it helps, guess what happens if you use `=>` with a `this`-aware function that *doesn't* need `var self = this` to work? You might be able to guess that it's going to mess things up. Yeah.

Consider:

```
var controller = {
    makeRequest: (..) => {
        // ..
        this.helper(..);
    },
    helper: (..) => {
        // ..
    }
};

controller.makeRequest(..);
```

Although we invoke as `controller.makeRequest(..)`, the `this.helper` reference fails, because `this` here doesn't point to con troller as it normally would. Where does it point? It lexically inherits `this` from the surrounding scope. In this previous snippet, that's the global scope, where `this` points to the global object. Ugh.

In addition to lexical `this`, arrow functions also have lexical `argu ments`—they don't have their own `arguments` array but instead inherit from their parent—as well as lexical `super` and `new.target` (see "Classes" on page 135 in Chapter 3).

So now we can conclude a more nuanced set of rules for when `=>` is appropriate and when it is not:

- If you have a short, single-statement inline function expression, where the only statement is a `return` of some computed value, *and* that function doesn't already make a `this` reference inside it, *and* there's no self-reference (recursion, event binding/unbinding), *and* you don't reasonably expect the function to ever be that way, you can probably safely refactor it to be an `=>` arrow function.

- If you have an inner function expression that's relying on a `var self = this` hack or a `.bind(this)` call on it in the enclosing function to ensure proper `this` binding, that inner function expression can probably safely become an `=>` arrow function.

- If you have an inner function expression that's relying on some-thing like `var args = Array.prototype.slice.call(argu ments)` in the enclosing function to make a lexical copy of `arguments`, that inner function expression can probably safely become an `=>` arrow function.

- For everything else—normal function declarations, longer mul-tistatement function expressions, functions that need a lexical name identifier self-reference (recursion, etc.), and any other function that doesn't fit the previous characteristics—you should probably avoid `=>` function syntax.

Bottom line: `=>` is about lexical binding of `this`, `arguments`, and `super`. These are intentional features designed to fix some common problems, not bugs, quirks, or mistakes in ES6.

Don't believe any hype that `=>` is primarily, or even mostly, about fewer keystrokes. Whether you save keystrokes or waste them, you should know exactly what you are intentionally doing with every character typed.

 If you have a function that for any of these articulated reasons is not a good match for an `=>` arrow function, but it's being declared as part of an object literal, recall from "Concise Methods" on page 39 earlier in this chapter that there's another option for shorter function syntax.

If you prefer a visual decision chart for how/why to pick an arrow function:

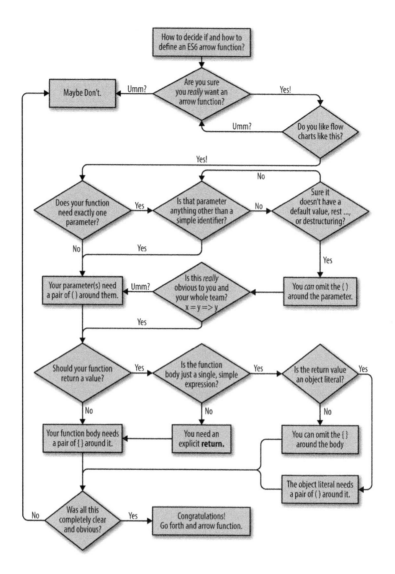

for..of Loops

Joining the `for` and `for..in` loops from the JavaScript we're all familiar with, ES6 adds a `for..of` loop, which loops over the set of values produced by an *iterator*.

The value you loop over with `for..of` must be an *iterable*, or it must be a value that can be coerced/boxed to an object (see the *Types &*

Grammar title of this series) that is an iterable. An iterable is simply an object that is able to produce an iterator, which the loop then uses.

Let's compare for..of to for..in to illustrate the difference:

```
var a = ["a","b","c","d","e"];

for (var idx in a) {
    console.log( idx );
}
// 0 1 2 3 4

for (var val of a) {
    console.log( val );
}
// "a" "b" "c" "d" "e"
```

As you can see, for..in loops over the keys/indexes in the a array, while for..of loops over the values in a.

Here's the pre-ES6 version of the for..of from that previous snippet:

```
var a = ["a","b","c","d","e"],
    k = Object.keys( a );

for (var val, i = 0; i < k.length; i++) {
    val = a[ k[i] ];
    console.log( val );
}
// "a" "b" "c" "d" "e"
```

And here's the ES6 but non-for..of equivalent, which also gives a glimpse at manually iterating an iterator (see "Iterators" on page 87 in Chapter 3):

```
var a = ["a","b","c","d","e"];

for (var val, ret, it = a[Symbol.iterator]();
    (ret = it.next()) && !ret.done;
) {
    val = ret.value;
    console.log( val );
}
// "a" "b" "c" "d" "e"
```

Under the covers, the for..of loop asks the iterable for an iterator (using the built-in Symbol.iterator; see "Well-Known Symbols" on page 203 in Chapter 7), then it repeatedly calls the iterator and assigns its produced value to the loop iteration variable.

Standard built-in values in JavaScript that are by default iterables (or provide them) include:

- Arrays
- Strings
- Generators (see Chapter 3)
- Collections / TypedArrays (see Chapter 5)

 Plain objects are not by default suitable for for..of looping. That's because they don't have a default iterator, which is intentional, not a mistake. However, we won't go any further into those nuanced reasonings here. In "Iterators" on page 87 in Chapter 3, we'll see how to define iterators for our own objects, which lets for..of loop over any object to get a set of values we define.

Here's how to loop over the characters in a primitive string:

```
for (var c of "hello") {
    console.log( c );
}
// "h" "e" "l" "l" "o"
```

The "hello" primitive string value is coerced/boxed to the String object wrapper equivalent, which is an iterable by default.

In for (XYZ of ABC).., the XYZ clause can either be an assignment expression or a declaration, identical to that same clause in for and for..in loops. So you can do stuff like this:

```
var o = {};

for (o.a of [1,2,3]) {
    console.log( o.a );
}
// 1 2 3

for ({x: o.a} of [ {x: 1}, {x: 2}, {x: 3} ]) {
  console.log( o.a );
```

```
}
// 1 2 3
```

for..of loops can be prematurely stopped, just like other loops, with break, continue, return (if in a function), and thrown exceptions. In any of these cases, the iterator's return(..) function is automatically called (if one exists) to let the iterator perform cleanup tasks, if necessary.

 See "Iterators" on page 87 in Chapter 3 for more complete coverage on iterables and iterators.

Regular Expressions

Let's face it: regular expressions haven't changed much in JS in a long time. So it's a great thing that they've finally learned a couple of new tricks in ES6. We'll briefly cover the additions here, but the overall topic of regular expressions is so dense that you'll need to turn to chapters/books dedicated to it (of which there are many!) if you need a refresher.

Unicode Flag

We'll cover the topic of Unicode in more detail in "Unicode" on page 73 later in this chapter. Here, we'll just look briefly at the new u flag for ES6+ regular expressions, which turns on Unicode matching for that expression.

JavaScript strings are typically interpreted as sequences of 16-bit characters, which correspond to the characters in the *Basic Multilingual Plane (BMP)* (*http://en.wikipedia.org/wiki/Plane_%28Unicode%29*). But there are many UTF-16 characters that fall outside this range, and so strings may have these multibyte characters in them.

Prior to ES6, regular expressions could only be matched based on BMP characters, which means that those extended characters were treated as two separate characters for matching purposes. This is often not ideal.

So, as of ES6, the u flag tells a regular expression to process a string with the interpretation of Unicode (UTF-16) characters, such that such an extended character will be matched as a single entity.

 Despite the name implication, "UTF-16" doesn't strictly mean 16 bits. Modern Unicode uses 21 bits, and standards like UTF-8 and UTF-16 refer roughly to how many bits are used in the representation of a character.

An example (straight from the ES6 specification): 𝄞 the musical symbol G-clef) is Unicode point U+1D11E (0x1D11E).

If this character appears in a regular expression pattern (like /𝄞/), the standard BMP interpretation would be that it's two separate characters (0xD834 and 0xDD1E) to match with. But the new ES6 Unicode-aware mode means that /𝄞/u (or the escaped Unicode form /\u{1D11E}/u) will match "𝄞" in a string as a single matched character.

You might be wondering why this matters? In non-Unicode BMP mode, the pattern is treated as two separate characters, but would still find the match in a string with the "𝄞" character in it, as you can see if you try:

```
/𝄞/.test( "𝄞-clef" );          // true
```

The length of the match is what matters. For example:

```
/^.-clef/ .test( "𝄞-clef" );     // false
/^.-clef/u.test( "𝄞-clef" );     // true
```

The ^.-clef in the pattern says to match only a single character at the beginning before the normal "-clef" text. In standard BMP mode, the match fails (two characters), but with u Unicode mode flagged on, the match succeeds (one character).

It's also important to note that u makes quantifiers like + and * apply to the entire Unicode code point as a single character, not just the *lower surrogate* (aka rightmost half of the symbol) of the character. The same goes for Unicode characters appearing in character classes, like /[♨-♻]/u.

There's plenty more nitty-gritty details about u behavior in regular expressions, which Mathias Bynens (*https://twitter.com/mathias*) has written extensively about (*https://mathiasbynens.be/notes/es6-unicode-regex*).

Sticky Flag

Another flag mode added to ES6 regular expressions is y, which is often called "sticky mode." *Sticky* essentially means the regular expression has a virtual anchor at its beginning that keeps it rooted to matching at only the position indicated by the regular expression's lastIndex property.

To illustrate, let's consider two regular expressions—the first without sticky mode and the second with:

```
var re1 = /foo/,
    str = "++foo++";

re1.lastIndex;          // 0
re1.test( str );        // true
re1.lastIndex;          // 0--not updated

re1.lastIndex = 4;
re1.test( str );        // true--ignored `lastIndex`
re1.lastIndex;          // 4--not updated
```

Three things to observe about this snippet:

- test(..) doesn't pay any attention to lastIndex's value, and always just performs its match from the beginning of the input string.

- Because our pattern does not have a ^ start-of-input anchor, the search for "foo" is free to move ahead through the whole string looking for a match.

- lastIndex is not updated by test(..).

Now, let's try a sticky mode regular expression:

```
var re2 = /foo/y,       // <-- notice the `y` sticky flag
    str = "++foo++";

re2.lastIndex;          // 0
re2.test( str );        // false--"foo" not found at `0`
re2.lastIndex;          // 0
```

```
re2.lastIndex = 2;
re2.test( str );        // true
re2.lastIndex;          // 5--updated to after previous match

re2.test( str );        // false
re2.lastIndex;          // 0--reset after previous match failure
```

And so our new observations about sticky mode:

- test(..) uses lastIndex as the exact and only position in str to look to make a match. There is no moving ahead to look for the match—it's either there at the lastIndex position or not.

- If a match is made, test(..) updates lastIndex to point to the character immediately following the match. If a match fails, test(..) resets lastIndex back to 0.

Normal nonsticky patterns that aren't otherwise ^-rooted to the start-of-input are free to move ahead in the input string looking for a match. But sticky mode restricts the pattern to matching just at the position of lastIndex.

As I suggested at the beginning of this section, another way of looking at this is that y implies a virtual anchor at the beginning of the pattern that is relative (aka constrains the start of the match) to exactly the lastIndex position.

 In previous literature on the topic, it has alternatively been asserted that this behavior is like y implying a ^ (start-of-input) anchor in the pattern. This is inaccurate. We'll explain in further detail in "Anchored Sticky" on page 70.

Sticky Positioning

It may seem strangely limiting that to use y for repeated matches, you have to manually ensure lastIndex is in the exact right position, as it has no move-ahead capability for matching.

Here's one possible scenario: if you know that the match you care about is always going to be at a position that's a multiple of a number (e.g., 0, 10, 20, etc.), you can just construct a limited pattern matching what you care about, but then manually set lastIndex each time before matching to those fixed positions.

Consider:

```
var re = /f../y,
    str = "foo        far        fad";

str.match( re );        // ["foo"]

re.lastIndex = 10;
str.match( re );        // ["far"]

re.lastIndex = 20;
str.match( re );        // ["fad"]
```

However, if you're parsing a string that isn't formatted in fixed positions like that, figuring out what to set lastIndex to before each match is likely going to be untenable.

There's a saving nuance to consider here. y requires that lastIndex be in the exact position for a match to occur. But it doesn't strictly require that *you* manually set lastIndex.

Instead, you can construct your expressions in such a way that they capture in each main match everything before and after the thing you care about, up to right before the next thing you'll care to match.

Because lastIndex will set to the next character beyond the end of a match, if you've matched everything up to that point, lastIndex will always be in the correct position for the y pattern to start from the next time.

 If you can't predict the structure of the input string in a sufficiently patterned way like that, this technique may not be suitable and you may not be able to use y.

Having structured string input is likely the most practical scenario where y will be capable of performing repeated matching throughout a string. Consider:

```
var re = /\d+\.\s(.*?)(?:\s|$)/y
    str = "1. foo 2. bar 3. baz";

str.match( re );        // [ "1. foo ", "foo" ]

re.lastIndex;           // 7--correct position!
str.match( re );        // [ "2. bar ", "bar" ]
```

```
re.lastIndex;              // 14--correct position!
str.match( re );           // ["3. baz", "baz"]
```

This works because I knew something ahead of time about the structure of the input string: there is always a numeral prefix like "1. " before the desired match ("foo", etc.), and either a space after it, or the end of the string ($ anchor). So the regular expression I constructed captures all of that in each main match, and then I use a matching group ( ) so that the stuff I really care about is separated out for convenience.

After the first match ("1. foo "), the lastIndex is 7, which is already the position needed to start the next match, for "2. bar ", and so on.

If you're going to use y sticky mode for repeated matches, you'll probably want to look for opportunities to have lastIndex automatically positioned as we've just demonstrated.

Sticky Versus Global

Some readers may be aware that you can emulate something like this lastIndex-relative matching with the g global match flag and the exec(..) method, as so:

```
var re = /o+./g,           // <-- look, `g`!
    str = "foot book more";

re.exec( str );            // ["oot"]
re.lastIndex;              // 4

re.exec( str );            // ["ook"]
re.lastIndex;              // 9

re.exec( str );            // ["or"]
re.lastIndex;              // 13

re.exec( str );            // null--no more matches!
re.lastIndex;              // 0--starts over now!
```

While it's true that g pattern matches with exec(..) start their matching from lastIndex's current value, and also update lastIndex after each match (or failure), this is not the same thing as y's behavior.

Notice in the previous snippet that "ook", located at position 6, was matched and found by the second exec(..) call, even though at the time, lastIndex was 4 (from the end of the previous match). Why? Because as we said earlier, nonsticky matches are free to move ahead in their matching. A sticky mode expression would have failed here, because it would not be allowed to move ahead.

In addition to perhaps undesired move-ahead matching behavior, another downside to just using g instead of y is that g changes the behavior of some matching methods, like str.match(re).

Consider:

```
var re = /o+./g,        // <-- look, `g`!
    str = "foot book more";

str.match( re );        // ["oot","ook","or"]
```

See how all the matches were returned at once? Sometimes that's OK, but sometimes that's not what you want.

The y sticky flag will give you one-at-a-time progressive matching with utilities like test(..) and match(..). Just make sure the lastIndex is always in the right position for each match!

Anchored Sticky

As we warned earlier, it's inaccurate to think of sticky mode as implying a pattern starts with ^. The ^ anchor has a distinct meaning in regular expressions, which is *not altered* by sticky mode. ^ is an anchor that *always* refers to the beginning of the input, and *is not* in any way relative to lastIndex.

Besides poor/inaccurate documentation on this topic, the confusion is unfortunately strengthened further because an older pre-ES6 experiment with sticky mode in Firefox *did* make ^ relative to lastIndex, so that behavior has been around for years.

ES6 elected not to do it that way. ^ in a pattern means start-of-input absolutely and only.

As a consequence, a pattern like /^foo/y will always and only find a "foo" match at the beginning of a string, *if it's allowed to match there*. If lastIndex is not 0, the match will fail. Consider:

```
var re = /^foo/y,
    str = "foo";

re.test( str );         // true
re.test( str );         // false
```

```
re.lastIndex;                // 0--reset after failure

re.lastIndex = 1;
re.test( str );              // false--failed for positioning
re.lastIndex;                // 0--reset after failure
```

Bottom line: y plus ^ plus `lastIndex` > 0 is an incompatible combination that will always cause a failed match.

 While y does not alter the meaning of ^ in any way, the m multiline mode *does*, such that ^ means start-of-input *or* start of text after a newline. So, if you combine y and m flags together for a pattern, you can find multiple ^-rooted matches in a string. But remember: because it's y sticky, you'll have to make sure `lastIndex` is pointing at the correct new line position (likely by matching to the end of the line) each subsequent time, or no subsequent matches will be made.

Regular Expression flags

Prior to ES6, if you wanted to examine a regular expression object to see what flags it had applied, you needed to parse them out—ironically, probably with another regular expression—from the content of the source property, such as:

```
var re = /foo/ig;

re.toString();               // "/foo/ig"

var flags = re.toString().match( /\/([gim]*)$/ )[1];

flags;                       // "ig"
```

As of ES6, you can now get these values directly, with the new flags property:

```
var re = /foo/ig;

re.flags;                    // "gi"
```

It's a small nuance, but the ES6 specification calls for the expression's flags to be listed in this order: "gimuy", regardless of what order the original pattern was specified with. That's the reason for the difference between /ig and "gi".

No, the order of flags specified or listed doesn't matter.

Another tweak from ES6 is that the `RegExp(..)` constructor is now `flags`-aware if you pass it an existing regular expression:

```
var re1 = /foo*/y;
re1.source;                    // "foo*"
re1.flags;                     // "y"

var re2 = new RegExp( re1 );
re2.source;                    // "foo*"
re2.flags;                     // "y"

var re3 = new RegExp( re1, "ig" );
re3.source;                    // "foo*"
re3.flags;                     // "gi"
```

Prior to ES6, the `re3` construction would throw an error, but as of ES6 you can override the flags when duplicating.

Number Literal Extensions

Prior to ES5, number literals looked like the following—the octal form was not officially specified, only allowed as an extension that browsers had come to de facto agreement on:

```
var dec = 42,
    oct = 052,
    hex = 0x2a;
```

> Though you are specifying a number in different bases, the number's mathematic value is what is stored, and the default output interpretation is always base-10. The three variables in the previous snippet all have the 42 value stored in them.

To further illustrate that `052` was a nonstandard form extension, consider:

```
Number( "42" );         // 42
Number( "052" );        // 52
Number( "0x2a" );       // 42
```

ES5 continued to permit the browser-extended octal form (including such inconsistencies), except that in strict mode, the octal literal (`052`) form is disallowed. This restriction was done mainly because many developers had the habit (from other languages) of seemingly

---

innocuously prefixing otherwise base-10 numbers with `0`s for code alignment purposes, and then running into the accidental fact that they'd changed the number value entirely!

ES6 continues the legacy of changes/variations to how number literals outside base-10 numbers can be represented. There's now an official octal form, an amended hexadecimal form, and a brand-new binary form. For web compatibility reasons, the old octal 052 form will continue to be legal (though unspecified) in nonstrict mode, but should really never be used anymore.

Here are the new ES6 number literal forms:

```
var dec = 42,
    oct = 0o52,        // or `0052` :(
    hex = 0x2a,        // or `0X2a` :/
    bin = 0b101010;    // or `0B101010` :/
```

The only decimal form allowed is base-10. Octal, hexadecimal, and binary are all integer forms.

And the string representations of these forms are all able to be coerced/converted to their number equivalent:

```
Number( "42" );          // 42
Number( "0o52" );        // 42
Number( "0x2a" );        // 42
Number( "0b101010" );    // 42
```

Though not strictly new to ES6, it's a little-known fact that you can actually go the opposite direction of conversion (well, sort of):

```
var a = 42;

a.toString();        // "42"--also `a.toString( 10 )`
a.toString( 8 );     // "52"
a.toString( 16 );    // "2a"
a.toString( 2 );     // "101010"
```

In fact, you can represent a number this way in any base from 2 to 36, though it'd be rare that you'd go outside the standard bases: 2, 8, 10, and 16.

Unicode

Let me just say that this section is not an exhaustive everything-you-ever-wanted-to-know-about-Unicode resource. I want to cover what you need to know that's *changing* for Unicode in ES6, but we won't go much deeper than that. Mathias Bynens (*http://twitter.com/mathias*) has written/spoken extensively and brilliantly about JS and Unicode (see *https://mathiasbynens.be/notes/javascript-unicode* and *http://fluentconf.com/javascript-html-2015/public/content/2015/02/18-javascript-loves-unicode*).

The Unicode characters that range from `0x0000` to `0xFFFF` contain all the standard printed characters (in various languages) that you're likely to have seen or interacted with. This group of characters is called the *Basic Multilingual Plane (BMP)*. The BMP even contains fun symbols like this cool snowman: ☃ (U+2603).

There are lots of other extended Unicode characters beyond this BMP set, which range up to `0x10FFFF`. These symbols are often referred to as *astral* symbols, as that's the name given to the set of 16 *planes* (e.g., layers/groupings) of characters beyond the BMP. Examples of astral symbols include 𝄞 U+1D11E) and 💩 U+1F4A9).

Prior to ES6, JavaScript strings could specify Unicode characters using Unicode escaping, such as:

```
var snowman = "\u2603";
console.log( snowman );          // "☃"
```

However, the `\uXXXX` Unicode escaping only supports four hexadecimal characters, so you can only represent the BMP set of characters in this way. To represent an astral character using Unicode escaping prior to ES6, you need to use a *surrogate pair*—basically two specially calculated Unicode-escaped characters side by side, which JS interprets together as a single astral character:

```
var gclef = "\uD834\uDD1E";
console.log( gclef );          // "𝄞"
```

As of ES6, we now have a new form for Unicode escaping (in strings and regular expressions), called Unicode *code point escaping*:

```
var gclef = "\u{1D11E}";
console.log( gclef );          // "𝄞"
```

As you can see, the difference is the presence of the { } in the escape sequence, which allows it to contain any number of hexadecimal characters. Because you only need six to represent the highest possible code point value in Unicode (i.e., 0x10FFFF), this is sufficient.

Unicode-Aware String Operations

By default, JavaScript string operations and methods are not sensitive to astral symbols in string values. So, they treat each BMP character individually, even the two surrogate halves that make up an otherwise single astral character. Consider:

```
var snowman = "☃";
snowman.length;                 // 1

var gclef = "𝄞";
gclef.length;                   // 2
```

So, how do we accurately calculate the length of such a string? In this scenario, the following trick will work:

```
var gclef = "𝄞";

[...gclef].length;              // 1
Array.from( gclef ).length;     // 1
```

Recall from "for..of Loops" on page 61 earlier in this chapter that ES6 strings have built-in iterators. This iterator happens to be Unicode-aware, meaning it will automatically output an astral symbol as a single value. We take advantage of that using the ... spread operator in an array literal, which creates an array of the string's symbols. Then we just inspect the length of that resultant array. ES6's `Array.from(..)` does basically the same thing as `[...XYZ]`, but we'll cover that utility in detail in Chapter 6.

It should be noted that constructing and exhausting an iterator just to get the length of a string is quite expensive on performance, relatively speaking, compared to what a theoretically optimized native utility/property would do.

Unfortunately, the full answer is not as simple or straightforward. In addition to the surrogate pairs (which the string iterator takes care of), there are special Unicode code points that behave in other special ways, which is much harder to account for. For example, there's a set of code points that modify the previous adjacent character, known as *Combining Diacritical Marks*.

Consider these two string outputs:

```
console.log( s1 );              // "é"
console.log( s2 );              // "é"
```

They look the same, but they're not! Here's how we created s1 and s2:

```
var s1 = "\xE9",
    s2 = "e\u0301";
```

As you can probably guess, our previous `length` trick doesn't work with s2:

```
[...s1].length;              // 1
[...s2].length;              // 2
```

So what can we do? In this case, we can perform a *Unicode normalization* on the value before inquiring about its length, using the ES6 `String#normalize(..)` utility (which we'll cover more in Chapter 6):

```
var s1 = "\xE9",
    s2 = "e\u0301";

s1.normalize().length;       // 1
s2.normalize().length;       // 1

s1 === s2;                   // false
s1 === s2.normalize();       // true
```

Essentially, `normalize(..)` takes a sequence like `"e\u0301"` and normalizes it to `"\xE9"`. Normalization can even combine multiple adjacent combining marks if there's a suitable Unicode character they combine to:

```
var s1 = "o\u0302\u0300",
    s2 = s1.normalize(),
    s3 = "ồ";

s1.length;                   // 3
s2.length;                   // 1
s3.length;                   // 1

s2 === s3;                   // true
```

Unfortunately, normalization isn't fully perfect here, either. If you have multiple combining marks modifying a single character, you may not get the length count you'd expect, because there may not be a single defined normalized character that represents the combination of all the marks. For example:

```
var s1 = "e\u0301\u0330";

console.log( s1 );           // "ḝ"
```

```
s1.normalize().length;          // 2
```

The further you go down this rabbit hole, the more you realize that it's difficult to get one precise definition for "length." What we see visually rendered as a single character—more precisely called a *grapheme*—doesn't always strictly relate to a single "character" in the program processing sense.

If you want to see just how deep this rabbit hole goes, check out the "Grapheme Cluster Boundaries" algorithm (*http://www.Unicode.org/ reports/tr29/#Grapheme_Cluster_Boundaries*).

Character Positioning

Similar to length complications, what does it actually mean to ask, "what is the character at position 2?" The naive pre-ES6 answer comes from charAt(..), which will not respect the atomicity of an astral character, nor will it take into account combining marks.

Consider:

```
var s1 = "abc\u0301d",
    s2 = "ab\u0107d",
    s3 = "ab\u{1d49e}d";

console.log( s1 );          // "abćd"
console.log( s2 );          // "abćd"
console.log( s3 );          // "ab𝒞d"

s1.charAt( 2 );             // "c"
s2.charAt( 2 );             // "ć"
s3.charAt( 2 );             // "" <-- unprintable surrogate
s3.charAt( 3 );             // "" <-- unprintable surrogate
```

So, is ES6 giving us a Unicode-aware version of charAt(..)? Unfortunately, no. At the time of this writing, there's a proposal for such a utility that's under consideration for post-ES6.

But with what we explored in the previous section (and of course with the limitations noted thereof!), we can hack an ES6 answer:

```
var s1 = "abc\u0301d",
    s2 = "ab\u0107d",
    s3 = "ab\u{1d49e}d";

[...s1.normalize()][2];          // "ć"
```

```
[...s2.normalize()][2];          // "ć"
[...s3.normalize()][2];          // "𝒞"
```

 Reminder of an earlier warning: constructing
and exhausting an iterator each time you want
to get at a single character is... very not ideal,
performance-wise. Let's hope we get a built-in
and optimized utility for this soon, post-ES6.

What about a Unicode-aware version of the charCodeAt(..) utility?
ES6 gives us codePointAt(..):

```
var s1 = "abc\u0301d",
    s2 = "ab\u0107d",
    s3 = "ab\u{1d49e}d";

s1.normalize().codePointAt( 2 ).toString( 16 );
// "107"

s2.normalize().codePointAt( 2 ).toString( 16 );
// "107"

s3.normalize().codePointAt( 2 ).toString( 16 );
// "1d49e"
```

What about the other direction? A Unicode-aware version of
String.fromCharCode(..) is ES6's String.fromCodePoint(..):

```
String.fromCodePoint( 0x107 );        // "ć"

String.fromCodePoint( 0x1d49e );      // "𝒞"
```

So wait, can we just combine String.fromCodePoint(..) and code
PointAt(..) to get a better version of a Unicode-aware charAt(..)
from earlier? Yep!

```
var s1 = "abc\u0301d",
    s2 = "ab\u0107d",
    s3 = "ab\u{1d49e}d";

String.fromCodePoint( s1.normalize().codePointAt( 2 ) );
// "ć"

String.fromCodePoint( s2.normalize().codePointAt( 2 ) );
// "ć"

String.fromCodePoint( s3.normalize().codePointAt( 2 ) );
// "𝒞"
```

```
```

There's quite a few other string methods we haven't addressed here, including `toUpperCase()`, `toLowerCase()`, `substring(..)`, `indexOf(..)`, `slice(..)`, and a dozen others. None of these have been changed or augmented for full Unicode awareness, so you should be very careful—probably just avoid them!—when working with strings containing astral symbols.

There are also several string methods that use regular expressions for their behavior, like `replace(..)` and `match(..)`. Thankfully, ES6 brings Unicode awareness to regular expressions, as we covered in "Unicode Flag" on page 64.

OK, there we have it! JavaScript's Unicode string support is significantly better over pre-ES6 (though still not perfect) with the various additions we've just covered.

Unicode Identifier Names

Unicode can also be used in identifier names (variables, properties, etc.). Prior to ES6, you could do this with Unicode-escapes, like:

```
var \u03A9 = 42;

// same as: var Ω = 42;
```

As of ES6, you can also use the earlier explained code point escape syntax:

```
var \u{2B400} = 42;

// same as: var 𫐀 = 42;
```

There's a complex set of rules around exactly which Unicode characters are allowed. Furthermore, some are allowed only if they're not the first character of the identifier name.

 Mathias Bynens has a great post (*https://mathias bynens.be/notes/javascript-identifiers-es6*) on all the nitty-gritty details.

The reasons for using such unusual characters in identifier names are rather rare and academic. You typically won't be best served by writing code that relies on these esoteric capabilities.

Symbols

With ES6, for the first time in quite a while, a new primitive type has been added to JavaScript: the symbol. Unlike the other primitive types, however, symbols don't have a literal form.

Here's how you create a symbol:

```
var sym = Symbol( "some optional description" );

typeof sym;      // "symbol"
```

Some things to note:

- You cannot and should not use new with Symbol(..). It's not a constructor, nor are you producing an object.
- The parameter passed to Symbol(..) is optional. If passed, it should be a string that gives a friendly description for the symbol's purpose.
- The typeof output is a new value ("symbol") that is the primary way to identify a symbol.

The description, if provided, is solely used for the stringification representation of the symbol:

```
sym.toString();      // "Symbol(some optional description)"
```

Similar to how primitive string values are not instances of String, symbols are also not instances of Symbol. If, for some reason, you want to construct a boxed wrapper object form of a symbol value, you can do the following:

```
sym instanceof Symbol;      // false

var symObj = Object( sym );
symObj instanceof Symbol;      // true

symObj.valueOf() === sym;      // true
```

 symObj in this snippet is interchangeable with sym; either form can be used in all places symbols are utilized. There's not much reason to use the boxed wrapper object form (symObj) instead of the primitive form (sym). Keeping with similar advice for other primitives, it's probably best to prefer sym over symObj.

The internal value of a symbol itself—referred to as its name—is hidden from the code and cannot be obtained. You can think of this symbol value as an automatically generated, unique (within your application) string value.

But if the value is hidden and unobtainable, what's the point of having a symbol at all?

The main point of a symbol is to create a string-like value that can't collide with any other value. So, for example, consider using a symbol as a constant representing an event name:

```
const EVT_LOGIN = Symbol( "event.login" );
```

You'd then use EVT_LOGIN in place of a generic string literal like "event.login":

```
evthub.listen( EVT_LOGIN, function(data){
    // ..
} );
```

The benefit here is that EVT_LOGIN holds a value that cannot be duplicated (accidentally or otherwise) by any other value, so it is impossible for there to be any confusion of which event is being dispatched or handled.

Under the covers, the evthub utility assumed in the previous snippet would almost certainly be using the symbol value from the EVT_LOGIN argument directly as the property/key in some internal object (hash) that tracks event handlers. If evthub instead needed to use the symbol value as a real string, it would need to explicitly coerce with String(..) or toString(), as implicit string coercion of symbols is not allowed.

You may use a symbol directly as a property name/key in an object, such as a special property you want to treat as hidden or meta in usage. It's important to know that although you intend to treat it as such, it is not *actually* a hidden or untouchable property.

Consider this module that implements the *singleton* pattern behavior—that is, it only allows itself to be created once:

```
const INSTANCE = Symbol( "instance" );

function HappyFace() {
```

```
    if (HappyFace[INSTANCE]) return HappyFace[INSTANCE];

    function smile() { .. }

    return HappyFace[INSTANCE] = {
        smile: smile
    };
}

var me = HappyFace(),
    you = HappyFace();

me === you;                    // true
```

The INSTANCE symbol value here is a special, almost hidden, meta-like property stored statically on the HappyFace() function object.

It could alternatively have been a plain old property like __instance, and the behavior would have been identical. The usage of a symbol simply improves the metaprogramming style, keeping this INSTANCE property set apart from any other normal properties.

Symbol Registry

One mild downside to using symbols as in the last few examples is that the EVT_LOGIN and INSTANCE variables had to be stored in an outer scope (perhaps even the global scope), or otherwise somehow stored in a publicly available location, so that all parts of the code that need to use the symbols can access them.

To aid in organizing code with access to these symbols, you can create symbol values with the *global symbol registry*. For example:

```
const EVT_LOGIN = Symbol.for( "event.login" );

console.log( EVT_LOGIN );       // Symbol(event.login)
```

And:

```
function HappyFace() {
    const INSTANCE = Symbol.for( "instance" );

    if (HappyFace[INSTANCE]) return HappyFace[INSTANCE];

    // ..

    return HappyFace[INSTANCE] = { .. };
}
```

`Symbol.for(..)` looks in the global symbol registry to see if a symbol is already stored with the provided description text, and returns it if so. If not, it creates one to return. In other words, the global symbol registry treats symbol values, by description text, as singletons themselves.

But that also means that any part of your application can retrieve the symbol from the registry using `Symbol.for(..)`, as long as the matching description name is used.

Ironically, symbols are basically intended to replace the use of *magic strings* (arbitrary string values given special meaning) in your application. But you precisely use *magic* description string values to uniquely identify/locate them in the global symbol registry!

To avoid accidental collisions, you'll probably want to make your symbol descriptions quite unique. One easy way of doing that is to include prefix/context/namespacing information in them.

For example, consider a utility such as the following:

```
function extractValues(str) {
    var key = Symbol.for( "extractValues.parse" ),
        re = extractValues[key] ||
            /[^=&]+?=([^&]+?)(?=&|$)/g,
        values = [], match;

    while (match = re.exec( str )) {
        values.push( match[1] );
    }

    return values;
}
```

We use the magic string value `"extractValues.parse"` because it's quite unlikely that any other symbol in the registry would ever collide with that description.

If a user of this utility wants to override the parsing regular expression, they can also use the symbol registry:

```
extractValues[Symbol.for( "extractValues.parse" )] =
    /..some pattern../g;

extractValues( "..some string.." );
```

Aside from the assistance the symbol registry provides in globally storing these values, everything we're seeing here could have been done by just actually using the magic string `"extractVal ues.parse"` as the key, rather than the symbol. The improvements exist at the metaprogramming level more than the functional level.

You may have occasion to use a symbol value that has been stored in the registry to look up what description text (key) it's stored under. For example, you may need to signal to another part of your application how to locate a symbol in the registry because you cannot pass the symbol value itself.

You can retrieve a registered symbol's description text (key) using `Symbol.keyFor(..)`:

```
var s = Symbol.for( "something cool" );

var desc = Symbol.keyFor( s );
console.log( desc );            // "something cool"

// get the symbol from the registry again
var s2 = Symbol.for( desc );

s2 === s;                       // true
```

Symbols as Object Properties

If a symbol is used as a property/key of an object, it's stored in a special way so that the property will not show up in a normal enumeration of the object's properties:

```
var o = {
    foo: 42,
    [ Symbol( "bar" ) ]: "hello world",
    baz: true
};

Object.getOwnPropertyNames( o );    // [ "foo","baz" ]
```

To retrieve an object's symbol properties:

```
Object.getOwnPropertySymbols( o );  // [ Symbol(bar) ]
```

This makes it clear that a property symbol is not actually hidden or inaccessible, as you can always see it in the `Object.getOwnProperty Symbols(..)` list.

Built-In Symbols

ES6 comes with a number of predefined built-in symbols that expose various meta behaviors on JavaScript object values. However, these symbols are *not* registered in the global symbol registry, as one might expect.

Instead, they're stored as properties on the Symbol function object. For example, in "for..of Loops" on page 61 earlier in this chapter, we introduced the Symbol.iterator value:

```
var a = [1,2,3];

a[Symbol.iterator];          // native function
```

The specification uses the @@ prefix notation to refer to the built-in symbols, the most common ones being: @@iterator, @@toStringTag, @@toPrimitive. Several others are defined as well, though they probably won't be used as often.

 See "Well-Known Symbols" on page 203 in Chapter 7 for detailed information about how these built-in symbols are used for meta programming purposes.

Review

ES6 adds a heap of new syntax forms to JavaScript, so there's plenty to learn!

Most of these are designed to ease the pain points of common programming idioms, such as setting default values to function parameters and gathering the "rest" of the parameters into an array. Destructuring is a powerful tool for more concisely expressing assignments of values from arrays and nested objects.

While features like => arrow functions appear to also be all about shorter and nicer-looking syntax, they actually have very specific behaviors that you should intentionally use only in appropriate situations.

Expanded Unicode support, new tricks for regular expressions, and even a new primitive symbol type round out the syntactic evolution of ES6.

CHAPTER 3

Organization

It's one thing to write JS code, but it's another to properly organize it. Utilizing common patterns for organization and reuse goes a long way to improving the readability and understandability of your code. Remember: code is at least as much about communicating to other developers as it is about feeding the computer instructions.

ES6 has several important features that help significantly improve these patterns, including iterators, generators, modules, and classes.

Iterators

An *iterator* is a structured pattern for pulling information from a source in one-at-a-time fashion. This pattern has been found in programming for a long time. And to be sure, JS developers have been ad hoc designing and implementing iterators in JS programs since before anyone can remember, so it's not at all a new topic.

What ES6 has done is introduce an implicit standardized interface for iterators. Many of the built-in data structures in JavaScript will now expose an iterator implementing this standard. And you can also construct your own iterators adhering to the same standard, for maximal interoperability.

Iterators are a way of organizing ordered, sequential, pull-based consumption of data.

For example, you may implement a utility that produces a new unique identifier each time it's requested. Or you may produce an infinite series of values that rotate through a fixed list, in round-robin fashion. Or you could attach an iterator to a database query result to pull out new rows one at a time.

Although they have not commonly been used in JS in such a manner, iterators can also be thought of as controlling behavior one step at a time. This can be illustrated quite clearly when considering generators (see "Generators" on page 98 later in this chapter), though you can certainly do the same without generators.

Interfaces

At the time of this writing, ES6 section 25.1.1.2 (*https://people.mozilla.org/~jorendorff/es6-draft.html#sec-iterator-interface*) details the `Iterator` interface as having the following requirement:

```
Iterator [required]
    next() {method}: retrieves next IteratorResult
```

There are two optional members that some iterators are extended with:

```
Iterator [optional]
    return() {method}: stops iterator and returns IteratorResult
    throw() {method}: signals error and returns IteratorResult
```

The `IteratorResult` interface is specified as:

```
IteratorResult
    value {property}: current iteration value or final return
        value (optional if `undefined`)
    done {property}: boolean, indicates completion status
```

I call these interfaces implicit not because they're not explicitly called out in the specification—they are!—but because they're not exposed as direct objects accessible to code. JavaScript does not, in ES6, support any notion of "interfaces," so adherence for your own code is purely conventional. However, wherever JS expects an iterator—a `for..of` loop, for instance—what you provide must adhere to these interfaces or the code will fail.

There's also an `Iterable` interface, which describes objects that must be able to produce iterators:

```
Iterable
    @@iterator() {method}: produces an Iterator
```

If you recall from "Built-In Symbols" on page 85 in Chapter 2, @@iterator is the special built-in symbol representing the method that can produce iterator(s) for the object.

IteratorResult

The IteratorResult interface specifies that the return value from any iterator operation will be an object of the form:

```
{ value: .. , done: true / false }
```

Built-in iterators will always return values of this form, but more properties are, of course, allowed to be present on the return value, as necessary.

For example, a custom iterator may add additional metadata to the result object (e.g., where the data came from, how long it took to retrieve, cache expiration length, frequency for the appropriate next request, etc.).

 Technically, value is optional if it would otherwise be considered absent or unset, such as in the case of the value undefined. Because accessing res.value will produce undefined whether it's present with that value or absent entirely, the presence/absence of the property is more an implementation detail or an optimization (or both), rather than a functional issue.

next() Iteration

Let's look at an array, which is an iterable, and the iterator it can produce to consume its values:

```
var arr = [1,2,3];

var it = arr[Symbol.iterator]();

it.next();      // { value: 1, done: false }
it.next();      // { value: 2, done: false }
it.next();      // { value: 3, done: false }

it.next();      // { value: undefined, done: true }
```

Each time the method located at `Symbol.iterator` (see Chapter 2 and Chapter 7) is invoked on this `arr` value, it will produce a new fresh iterator. Most structures will do the same, including all the built-in data structures in JS.

However, a structure like an event queue consumer might only ever produce a single iterator (singleton pattern). Or a structure might only allow one unique iterator at a time, requiring the current one to be completed before a new one can be created.

The `it` iterator in the previous snippet doesn't report `done: true` when you receive the 3 value. You have to call `next()` again, in essence going beyond the end of the array's values, to get the complete signal `done: true`. It may not be clear why until later in this section, but that design decision will typically be considered a best practice.

Primitive string values are also iterables by default:

```
var greeting = "hello world";

var it = greeting[Symbol.iterator]();

it.next();      // { value: "h", done: false }
it.next();      // { value: "e", done: false }
..
```

 Technically, the primitive value itself isn't iterable, but thanks to "boxing", `"hello world"` is coerced/converted to its `String` object wrapper form, which *is* an iterable. See the *Types & Grammar* title of this series for more information.

ES6 also includes several new data structures, called collections (see Chapter 5). These collections are not only iterables themselves, but they also provide API method(s) to generate an iterator, such as:

```
var m = new Map();
m.set( "foo", 42 );
m.set( { cool: true }, "hello world" );

var it1 = m[Symbol.iterator]();
var it2 = m.entries();

it1.next();     // { value: [ "foo", 42 ], done: false }
```

```
it2.next();      // { value: [ "foo", 42 ], done: false }
..
```

The next(..) method of an iterator can optionally take one or more arguments. The built-in iterators mostly do not exercise this capability, though a generator's iterator definitely does (see "Generators" on page 98 later in this chapter).

By general convention, including all the built-in iterators, calling next(..) on an iterator that's already been exhausted is not an error, but will simply continue to return the result { value: undefined, done: true }.

Optional: return(..) and throw(..)

The optional methods on the iterator interface—return(..) and throw(..)—are not implemented on most of the built-in iterators. However, they definitely do mean something in the context of generators, so see "Generators" on page 98 for more specific information.

return(..) is defined as sending a signal to an iterator that the consuming code is complete and will not be pulling any more values from it. This signal can be used to notify the producer (the iterator responding to next(..) calls) to perform any cleanup it may need to do, such as releasing/closing network, database, or file handle resources.

If an iterator has a return(..) present and any condition occurs that can automatically be interpreted as abnormal or early termination of consuming the iterator, return(..) will automatically be called. You can call return(..) manually as well.

return(..) will return an IteratorResult object just like next(..) does. In general, the optional value you send to return(..) would be sent back as value in this IteratorResult, though there are nuanced cases where that might not be true.

throw(..) is used to signal an exception/error to an iterator, which possibly may be used differently by the iterator than the completion signal implied by return(..). It does not necessarily imply a complete stop of the iterator as return(..) generally does.

For example, with generator iterators, throw(..) actually injects a thrown exception into the generator's paused execution context, which can be caught with a `try..catch`. An uncaught `throw(..)` exception would end up abnormally aborting the generator's iterator.

 By general convention, an iterator should not produce any more results after having called `return(..)` or `throw(..)`.

Iterator Loop

As we covered in "for..of Loops" on page 61 in Chapter 2, the ES6 `for..of` loop directly consumes a conforming iterable.

If an iterator is also an iterable, it can be used directly with the `for..of` loop. You make an iterator an iterable by giving it a `Symbol.iterator` method that simply returns the iterator itself:

```
var it = {
    // make the `it` iterator an iterable
    [Symbol.iterator]() { return this; },

    next() { .. },
    ..
};

it[Symbol.iterator]() === it;        // true
```

Now we can consume the `it` iterator with a `for..of` loop:

```
for (var v of it) {
    console.log( v );
}
```

To fully understand how such a loop works, recall the `for` equivalent of a `for..of` loop from Chapter 2:

```
for (var v, res; (res = it.next()) && !res.done; ) {
    v = res.value;
    console.log( v );
}
```

If you look closely, you'll see that `it.next()` is called before each iteration, and then `res.done` is consulted. If `res.done` is `true`, the expression evaluates to `false` and the iteration doesn't occur.

Recall earlier that we suggested iterators should in general not return done: true along with the final intended value from the iterator. Now you can see why.

If an iterator returned { done: true, value: 42 }, the for..of loop would completely discard the 42 value and it'd be lost. For this reason, assuming that your iterator may be consumed by patterns like the for..of loop or its manual for equivalent, you should probably wait to return done: true for signaling completion until after you've already returned all relevant iteration values.

 You can, of course, intentionally design your iterator to return some relevant value at the same time as returning done: true. But don't do this unless you've documented that as the case, and thus implicitly forced consumers of your iterator to use a different pattern for iteration than is implied by for..of or its manual equivalent as we depicted.

Custom Iterators

In addition to the standard built-in iterators, you can make your own! All it takes to make them interoperate with ES6's consumption facilities (e.g., the for..of loop and the ... operator) is to adhere to the proper interface(s).

Let's try constructing an iterator that produces the infinite series of numbers in the Fibonacci sequence:

```
var Fib = {
    [Symbol.iterator]() {
        var n1 = 1, n2 = 1;

        return {
            // make the iterator an iterable
            [Symbol.iterator]() { return this; },

            next() {
                var current = n2;
                n2 = n1;
                n1 = n1 + current;
                return { value: current, done: false };
            },

            return(v) {
```

```
                console.log(
                    "Fibonacci sequence abandoned."
                );
                return { value: v, done: true };
            }
        };
    }
};

for (var v of Fib) {
    console.log( v );

    if (v > 50) break;
}
// 1 1 2 3 5 8 13 21 34 55
// Fibonacci sequence abandoned.
```

 If we hadn't inserted the break condition, this for..of loop would have run forever, which is probably not the desired result in terms of breaking your program!

The Fib[Symbol.iterator]() method when called returns the iterator object with next() and return(..) methods on it. State is maintained via n1 and n2 variables, which are kept by the closure.

Let's *next* consider an iterator that is designed to run through a series (aka a queue) of actions, one item at a time:

```
var tasks = {
    [Symbol.iterator]() {
        var steps = this.actions.slice();

        return {
            // make the iterator an iterable
            [Symbol.iterator]() { return this; },

            next(...args) {
                if (steps.length > 0) {
                    let res = steps.shift()( ...args );
                    return { value: res, done: false };
                }
                else {
                    return { done: true }
                }
            },

            return(v) {
                steps.length = 0;
```

```
                return { value: v, done: true };
            }
        };
    },
    actions: []
};
```

The iterator on `tasks` steps through functions found in the `actions` array property, if any, and executes them one at a time, passing in whatever arguments you pass to `next(..)`, and returning any return value to you in the standard `IteratorResult` object.

Here's how we could could use this `tasks` queue:

```
tasks.actions.push(
    function step1(x){
        console.log( "step 1:", x );
        return x * 2;
    },
    function step2(x,y){
        console.log( "step 2:", x, y );
        return x + (y * 2);
    },
    function step3(x,y,z){
        console.log( "step 3:", x, y, z );
        return (x * y) + z;
    }
);

var it = tasks[Symbol.iterator]();

it.next( 10 );              // step 1: 10
                           // { value:    20, done: false }

it.next( 20, 50 );         // step 2: 20 50
                           // { value:   120, done: false }

it.next( 20, 50, 120 ); // step 3: 20 50 120
                           // { value: 1120, done: false }

it.next();                 // { done: true }
```

This particular usage reinforces that iterators can be a pattern for organizing functionality, not just data. It's also reminiscent of what we'll see with generators in the next section.

You could even get creative and define an iterator that represents meta operations on a single piece of data. For example, we could define an iterator for numbers that by default ranges from 0 up to (or down to, for negative numbers) the number in question.

Consider:

```
if (!Number.prototype[Symbol.iterator]) {
    Object.defineProperty(
        Number.prototype,
        Symbol.iterator,
        {
            writable: true,
            configurable: true,
            enumerable: false,
            value: function iterator(){
                var i, inc, done = false, top = +this;

                // iterate positively or negatively?
                inc = 1 * (top < 0 ? -1 : 1);

                return {
                    // make the iterator itself an iterable!
                    [Symbol.iterator](){ return this; },

                    next() {
                        if (!done) {
                            // initial iteration always 0
                            if (i == null) {
                                i = 0;
                            }
                            // iterating positively
                            else if (top >= 0) {
                                i = Math.min(top,i + inc);
                            }
                            // iterating negatively
                            else {
                                i = Math.max(top,i + inc);
                            }

                            // done after this iteration?
                            if (i == top) done = true;

                            return { value: i, done: false };
                        }
                        else {
                            return { done: true };
                        }
                    }
                };
            }
        }
    );
}
```

Now, what tricks does this creativity afford us?

```
for (var i of 3) {
    console.log( i );
}
// 0 1 2 3

[...-3];                    // [0,-1,-2,-3]
```

Those are some fun tricks, though the practical utility is somewhat debatable. But then again, one might wonder why ES6 didn't just ship with such a minor but delightful feature easter egg!

I'd be remiss if I didn't at least remind you that extending native prototypes as I'm doing in the previous snippet is something you should only do with caution and awareness of potential hazards.

In this case, the chances that you'll have a collision with other code or even a future JS feature is probably exceedingly low. But just beware of the slight possibility. And document what you're doing verbosely for posterity's sake.

 I've expounded on this particular technique in this blog post (*http://blog.getify.com/iterating-es6-numbers/*) if you want more details. And this comment (*http://blog.getify.com/iterating-es6-numbers/comment-page-1/#comment-535294*) even suggests a similar trick but for making string character ranges.

Iterator Consumption

We've already shown consuming an iterator item by item with the for..of loop. But there are other ES6 structures that can consume iterators.

Let's consider the iterator attached to this array (though any iterator we choose would have the following behaviors):

```
var a = [1,2,3,4,5];
```

The ... spread operator fully exhausts an iterator. Consider:

```
function foo(x,y,z,w,p) {
    console.log( x + y + z + w + p );
}

foo( ...a );               // 15
```

... can also spread an iterator inside an array:

```
var b = [ 0, ...a, 6 ];
b;                           // [0,1,2,3,4,5,6]
```

Array destructuring (see "Destructuring" on page 23 in Chapter 2) can partially or completely (if paired with a ... rest/gather operator) consume an iterator:

```
var it = a[Symbol.iterator]();

var [x,y] = it;
// take just the first two elements from `it`
var [z, ...w] = it;
// take the third, then the rest all at once

// is `it` fully exhausted? Yep.
it.next();                   // { value: undefined, done: true }

x;                           // 1
y;                           // 2
z;                           // 3
w;                           // [4,5]
```

Generators

All functions run to completion, right? In other words, once a function starts running, it finishes before anything else can interrupt.

At least that's how it's been for the whole history of JavaScript up to this point. As of ES6, a new somewhat exotic form of function is being introduced, called a generator. A generator can pause itself in mid-execution, and can be resumed either right away or at a later time. So it clearly does not hold the run-to-completion guarantee that normal functions do.

Moreover, each pause/resume cycle in mid-execution is an opportunity for two-way message passing, where the generator can return a value, and the controlling code that resumes it can send a value back in.

As with iterators in the previous section, there are multiple ways to think about what a generator is, or rather what it's most useful for. There's no one right answer, but we'll try to consider several angles.

See the *Async & Performance* title of this series for more information about generators, and also see Chapter 4 of this current title.

Syntax

The generator function is declared with this new syntax:

```
function *foo() {
    // ..
}
```

The position of the * is not functionally relevant. The same declaration could be written as any of the following:

```
function *foo()  { .. }
function* foo()  { .. }
function * foo() { .. }
function*foo()   { .. }
..
```

The *only* difference here is stylistic preference. Most other literature seems to prefer `function*  foo(..)  {  ..  }`. I prefer `function *foo(..) { .. }`, so that's how I'll present them for the rest of this title.

My reason is purely didactic in nature. In this text, when referring to a generator function, I will use `*foo(..)`, as opposed to `foo(..)` for a normal function. I observe that `*foo(..)` more closely matches the * positioning of `function *foo(..) { .. }`.

Moreover, as we saw in Chapter 2 with concise methods, there's a concise generator form in object literals:

```
var a = {
    *foo() { .. }
};
```

I would say that with concise generators, `*foo() { .. }` is rather more natural than `* foo() { .. }`. So that further argues for matching the consistency with `*foo()`.

Consistency eases understanding and learning.

Executing a Generator

Though a generator is declared with *, you still execute it like a normal function:

```
foo();
```

You can still pass it arguments, as in:

```
function *foo(x,y) {
    // ..
}

foo( 5, 10 );
```

The major difference is that executing a generator, like foo(5,10), doesn't actually run the code in the generator. Instead, it produces an iterator that will control the generator to execute its code.

We'll come back to this later in "Iterator Control" on page 105, but briefly:

```
function *foo() {
    // ..
}

var it = foo();

// to start/advanced `*foo()`, call
// `it.next(..)`
```

yield

Generators also have a new keyword you can use inside them, to signal the pause point: yield. Consider:

```
function *foo() {
    var x = 10;
    var y = 20;

    yield;

    var z = x + y;
}
```

In this *foo() generator, the operations on the first two lines would run at the beginning, then yield would pause the generator. If and when resumed, the last line of *foo() would run. yield can appear any number of times (or not at all, technically!) in a generator.

You can even put yield inside a loop, and it can represent a repeated pause point. In fact, a loop that never completes just means a generator that never completes, which is completely valid, and sometimes entirely what you need.

yield is not just a pause point. It's an expression that sends out a value when pausing the generator. Here's a while..true loop in a generator that for each iteration yields a new random number:

```
function *foo() {
    while (true) {
        yield Math.random();
    }
}
```

The yield .. expression not only sends a value—yield without a value is the same as yield undefined—but also receives (i.e., is replaced by) the eventual resumption value. Consider:

```
function *foo() {
    var x = yield 10;
    console.log( x );
}
```

This generator will first yield out the value 10 when pausing itself. When you resume the generator—using the it.next(..) we referred to earlier—whatever value (if any) you resume with will replace/complete the whole yield 10 expression, meaning that the value will be assigned to the x variable.

A yield .. expression can appear anywhere a normal expression can. For example:

```
function *foo() {
    var arr = [ yield 1, yield 2, yield 3 ];
    console.log( arr, yield 4 );
}
```

*foo() here has four yield .. expressions. Each yield results in the generator pausing to wait for a resumption value that's then used in the various expression contexts.

yield is not technically an operator, though when used like yield 1 it sure looks like it. Because yield can be used all by itself as in var x = yield;, thinking of it as an operator can sometimes be confusing.

Technically, yield .. is of the same "expression precedence"—similar conceptually to operator precedence—as an assignment expression like a = 3. That means yield .. can basically appear anywhere a = 3 can validly appear.

Let's illustrate the symmetry:

```
var a, b;

a = 3;              // valid
b = 2 + a = 3;      // invalid
```

```
b = 2 + (a = 3);          // valid

yield 3;                  // valid
a = 2 + yield 3;          // invalid
a = 2 + (yield 3);        // valid
```

 If you think about it, it makes a sort of conceptual sense that a yield .. expression would behave similar to an assignment expression. When a paused yield expression is resumed, it's completed/replaced by the resumption value in a way that's not terribly dissimilar from being "assigned" that value.

The takeaway: if you need yield .. to appear in a position where an assignment like a = 3 would not itself be allowed, it needs to be wrapped in a ( ).

Because of the low precedence of the yield keyword, almost any expression after a yield .. will be computed first before being sent with yield. Only the ... spread operator and the , comma operator have lower precedence, meaning they'd bind after the yield has been evaluated.

So just like with multiple operators in normal statements, another case where ( ) might be needed is to override (elevate) the low precedence of yield, such as the difference between these expressions:

```
yield 2 + 3;              // same as `yield (2 + 3)`

(yield 2) + 3;            // `yield 2` first, then `+ 3`
```

Just like = assignment, yield is also "right-associative," which means that multiple yield expressions in succession are treated as having been (..) grouped from right to left. So, yield yield yield 3 is treated as yield (yield (yield 3)). A "left-associative" interpretation like ((yield) yield) yield 3 would make no sense.

Just like with operators, it's a good idea to use (..) grouping, even if not strictly required, to disambiguate your intent if yield is combined with other operators or yields.

See the *Types & Grammar* title of this series for more information about operator precedence and associativity.

yield *

In the same way that the * makes a function declaration into func tion * generator declaration, a * makes yield into yield *, which is a very different mechanism, called *yield delegation*. Grammatically, yield *.. will behave the same as a yield .., as discussed in the previous section.

yield * .. requires an iterable; it then invokes that iterable's iterator, and delegates its own host generator's control to that iterator until it's exhausted. Consider:

```
function *foo() {
    yield *[1,2,3];
}
```

As with the * position in a generator's declaration (discussed earlier), the * positioning in yield * expressions is stylistically up to you. Most other literature prefers yield* .., but I prefer yield *.., for very symmetrical reasons as already discussed.

The [1,2,3] value produces an iterator that will step through its values, so the *foo() generator will yield those values out as it's consumed. Another way to illustrate the behavior is in yield delegating to another generator:

```
function *foo() {
    yield 1;
    yield 2;
    yield 3;
}

function *bar() {
    yield *foo();
}
```

The iterator produced when *bar() calls *foo() is delegated to via yield *, meaning whatever value(s) *foo() produces will be produced by *bar().

Whereas with `yield ..` the completion value of the expression comes from resuming the generator with `it.next(..)`, the completion value of the `yield *..` expression comes from the return value (if any) from the delegated-to iterator.

Built-in iterators generally don't have return values, as we covered at the end of "Iterator Loop" on page 92 earlier in this chapter. But if you define your own custom iterator (or generator), you can design it to `return` a value, which `yield *..` would capture:

```
function *foo() {
    yield 1;
    yield 2;
    yield 3;
    return 4;
}

function *bar() {
    var x = yield *foo();
    console.log( "x:", x );
}

for (var v of bar()) {
    console.log( v );
}
// 1 2 3
// x: 4
```

While the 1, 2, and 3 values are `yield`ed out of `*foo()` and then out of `*bar()`, the 4 value returned from `*foo()` is the completion value of the `yield *foo()` expression, which then gets assigned to x.

Because `yield *` can call another generator (by way of delegating to its iterator), it can also perform a sort of generator recursion by calling itself:

```
function *foo(x) {
    if (x < 3) {
        x = yield *foo( x + 1 );
    }
    return x * 2;
}

foo( 1 );
```

The result from `foo(1)` and then calling the iterator's `next()` to run it through its recursive steps will be 24. The first `*foo(..)` run has x at value 1, which is x < 3. x + 1 is passed recursively to `*foo(..)`, so x is then 2. One more recursive call results in x of 3.

Now, because x < 3 fails, the recursion stops, and return 3 * 2 gives 6 back to the previous call's yield *.. expression, which is then assigned to x. Another return 6 * 2 returns 12 back to the previous call's x. Finally 12 * 2, or 24, is returned from the completed run of the *foo(..) generator.

Iterator Control

Earlier, we briefly introduced the concept that generators are controlled by iterators. Let's fully dig into that now.

Recall the recursive *foo(..) from the previous section. Here's how we'd run it:

```
function *foo(x) {
    if (x < 3) {
        x = yield *foo( x + 1 );
    }
    return x * 2;
}

var it = foo( 1 );
it.next();                  // { value: 24, done: true }
```

In this case, the generator doesn't really ever pause, as there's no yield .. expression. Instead, yield * just keeps the current iteration step going via the recursive call. So, just one call to the iterator's next() function fully runs the generator.

Now let's consider a generator that will have multiple steps and thus multiple produced values:

```
function *foo() {
    yield 1;
    yield 2;
    yield 3;
}
```

We already know we can consume an iterator, even one attached to a generator like *foo(), with a for..of loop:

```
for (var v of foo()) {
    console.log( v );
}
// 1 2 3
```

The for..of loop requires an iterable. A generator function reference (like foo) by itself is not an iterable; you must execute it with foo() to get the iterator (which is also an iterable, as we explained earlier in this chapter). You could theoretically extend the GeneratorPrototype (the prototype of all generator functions) with a Symbol.iterator function that essentially just does return this(). That would make the foo reference itself an iterable, which means for (var v of foo) { .. } (notice no () on foo) will work.

Let's instead iterate the generator manually:

```
function *foo() {
    yield 1;
    yield 2;
    yield 3;
}

var it = foo();

it.next();          // { value: 1, done: false }
it.next();          // { value: 2, done: false }
it.next();          // { value: 3, done: false }

it.next();          // { value: undefined, done: true }
```

If you look closely, there are three yield statements and four next() calls. That may seem like a strange mismatch. In fact, there will always be one more next() call than yield expression, assuming all are evaluated and the generator is fully run to completion.

But if you look at it from the opposite perspective (inside-out instead of outside-in), the matching between yield and next() makes more sense.

Recall that the yield .. expression will be completed by the value you resume the generator with. That means the argument you pass to next(..) completes whatever yield .. expression is currently paused waiting for a completion.

Let's illustrate this perspective this way:

```
function *foo() {
    var x = yield 1;
    var y = yield 2;
```

```
    var z = yield 3;
    console.log( x, y, z );
}
```

In this snippet, each `yield` .. is sending a value out (1, 2, 3), but more directly, it's pausing the generator to wait for a value. In other words, it's almost like asking the question, "What value should I use here? I'll wait to hear back."

Now, here's how we control `*foo()` to start it up:

```
var it = foo();

it.next();                // { value: 1, done: false }
```

That first `next()` call is starting up the generator from its initial paused state, and running it to the first `yield`. At the moment you call that first `next()`, there's no `yield` .. expression waiting for a completion. If you passed a value to that first `next()` call, it would currently just be thrown away, because no `yield` is waiting to receive such a value.

An early proposal for the "beyond ES6" time-frame *would* let you access a value passed to an initial `next(..)` call via a separate meta property (see Chapter 7) inside the generator.

Now, let's answer the currently pending question, "What value should I assign to x?" We'll answer it by sending a value to the *next* `next(..)` call:

```
it.next( "foo" );         // { value: 2, done: false }
```

Now, the `x` will have the value `"foo"`, but we've also asked a new question, "What value should I assign to y?" And we answer:

```
it.next( "bar" );         // { value: 3, done: false }
```

Answer given, another question asked. Final answer:

```
it.next( "baz" );         // "foo" "bar" "baz"
                          // { value: undefined, done: true }
```

Now it should be clearer how each `yield` .. "question" is answered by the *next* `next(..)` call, and so the "extra" `next()` call we observed is always just the initial one that starts everything going.

Let's put all those steps together:

```
var it = foo();

// start up the generator
it.next();                // { value: 1, done: false }

// answer first question
it.next( "foo" );         // { value: 2, done: false }

// answer second question
it.next( "bar" );         // { value: 3, done: false }

// answer third question
it.next( "baz" );         // "foo" "bar" "baz"
                          // { value: undefined, done: true }
```

You can think of a generator as a producer of values, in which case each iteration is simply producing a value to be consumed.

But in a more general sense, perhaps it's appropriate to think of generators as controlled, progressive code execution, much like the tasks queue example from the earlier section "Custom Iterators" on page 93.

 That perspective is exactly the motivation for how we'll revisit generators in Chapter 4. Specifically, there's no reason that next(..) has to be called right away after the previous next(..) finishes. While the generator's inner execution context is paused, the rest of the program continues unblocked, including the ability for asynchronous actions to control when the generator is resumed.

Early Completion

As we covered earlier in this chapter, the iterator attached to a generator supports the optional return(..) and throw(..) methods. Both of them have the effect of aborting a paused generator immediately.

Consider:

```
function *foo() {
    yield 1;
    yield 2;
    yield 3;
}
```

```
var it = foo();

it.next();              // { value: 1, done: false }

it.return( 42 );        // { value: 42, done: true }

it.next();              // { value: undefined, done: true }
```

return(x) is kind of like forcing a return x to be processed at exactly that moment, such that you get the specified value right back. Once a generator is completed, either normally or early as shown, it no longer processes any code or returns any values.

In addition to return(..) being callable manually, it's also called automatically at the end of iteration by any of the ES6 constructs that consume iterators, such as the for..of loop and the ... spread operator.

The purpose of this capability is to notify the generator if the controlling code is no longer going to iterate over it anymore, so that it can perhaps do any cleanup tasks (freeing up resources, resetting status, etc.). Identical to a normal function cleanup pattern, the main way to accomplish this is to use a finally clause:

```
function *foo() {
    try {
        yield 1;
        yield 2;
        yield 3;
    }
    finally {
        console.log( "cleanup!" );
    }
}

for (var v of foo()) {
    console.log( v );
}
// 1 2 3
// cleanup!

var it = foo();

it.next();              // { value: 1, done: false }
it.return( 42 );        // cleanup!
                        // { value: 42, done: true }
```

Do not put a yield statement inside the finally clause! It's valid and legal, but it's a really terrible idea. It acts in a sense as deferring the completion of the return(..) call you made, as any yield .. expressions in the finally clause are respected to pause and send messages; you don't immediately get a completed generator as expected. There's basically no good reason to opt in to that crazy *bad part*, so avoid doing so!

In addition to the previous snippet showing how return(..) aborts the generator while still triggering the finally clause, it also demonstrates that a generator produces a whole new iterator each time it's called. In fact, you can use multiple iterators attached to the same generator concurrently:

```
function *foo() {
    yield 1;
    yield 2;
    yield 3;
}

var it1 = foo();
it1.next();             // { value: 1, done: false }
it1.next();             // { value: 2, done: false }

var it2 = foo();
it2.next();             // { value: 1, done: false }

it1.next();             // { value: 3, done: false }

it2.next();             // { value: 2, done: false }
it2.next();             // { value: 3, done: false }

it2.next();             // { value: undefined, done: true }
it1.next();             // { value: undefined, done: true }
```

Early Abort

Instead of calling return(..), you can call throw(..). Just like return(x) is essentially injecting a return x into the generator at its current pause point, calling throw(x) is essentially like injecting a throw x at the pause point.

Other than the exception behavior (we cover what that means to try clauses in the next section), throw(..) produces the same sort of

---

early completion that aborts the generator's run at its current pause point. For example:

```
function *foo() {
    yield 1;
    yield 2;
    yield 3;
}

var it = foo();

it.next();                 // { value: 1, done: false }

try {
    it.throw( "Oops!" );
}
catch (err) {
    console.log( err ); // Exception: Oops!
}

it.next();                 // { value: undefined, done: true }
```

Because throw(..) basically injects a throw .. in replacement of the yield 1 line of the generator, and nothing handles this exception, it immediately propagates back out to the calling code, which handles it with a try..catch.

Unlike return(..), the iterator's throw(..) method is never called automatically.

Of course, though not shown in the previous snippet, if a try..finally clause was waiting inside the generator when you call throw(..), the finally clause would be given a chance to complete before the exception is propagated back to the calling code.

Error Handling

As we've already hinted, error handling with generators can be expressed with try..catch, which works in both inbound and outbound directions:

```
function *foo() {
    try {
        yield 1;
    }
    catch (err) {
        console.log( err );
    }
```

```
    yield 2;

    throw "Hello!";
}

var it = foo();

it.next();                  // { value: 1, done: false }

try {
    it.throw( "Hi!" );   // Hi!
                          // { value: 2, done: false }
    it.next();

    console.log( "never gets here" );
}
catch (err) {
    console.log( err ); // Hello!
}
```

Errors can also propagate in both directions through yield * delegation:

```
function *foo() {
    try {
        yield 1;
    }
    catch (err) {
        console.log( err );
    }

    yield 2;

    throw "foo: e2";
}

function *bar() {
    try {
        yield *foo();

        console.log( "never gets here" );
    }
    catch (err) {
        console.log( err );
    }
}

var it = bar();

try {
    it.next();                  // { value: 1, done: false }
```

```
    it.throw( "e1" );    // e1
                         // { value: 2, done: false }

    it.next();           // foo: e2
                         // { value: undefined, done: true }
}
catch (err) {
    console.log( "never gets here" );
}

it.next();                // { value: undefined, done: true }
```

When *foo() calls yield 1, the 1 value passes through *bar() untouched, as we've already seen.

But what's most interesting about this snippet is that when *foo() calls throw "foo: e2", this error propagates to *bar() and is immediately caught by *bar()'s try..catch block. The error doesn't pass through *bar() like the 1 value did.

*bar()'s catch then does a normal output of err ("foo: e2") and then *bar() finishes normally, which is why the { value: unde fined, done: true } iterator result comes back from it.next().

If *bar() didn't have a try..catch around the yield *.. expression, the error would of course propagate all the way out, and on the way through it still would complete (abort) *bar().

Transpiling a Generator

Is it possible to represent a generator's capabilities prior to ES6? It turns out it is, and there are several great tools that do so, including most notably Facebook's Regenerator tool (*https://facebook.github.io/regenerator/*).

But just to better understand generators, let's try our hand at manually converting. Basically, we're going to create a simple closure-based state machine.

We'll keep our source generator really simple:

```
function *foo() {
    var x = yield 42;
    console.log( x );
}
```

To start, we'll need a function called `foo()` that we can execute, which needs to return an iterator:

```
function foo() {
    // ..

    return {
        next: function(v) {
            // ..
        }

        // we'll skip `return(..)` and `throw(..)`
    };
}
```

Now, we need some inner variable to keep track of where we are in the steps of our "generator"'s logic. We'll call it `state`. There will be three states: 0 initially, 1 while waiting to fulfill the `yield` expression, and 2 once the generator is complete.

Each time `next(..)` is called, we need to process the next step, and then increment `state`. For convenience, we'll put each step into a `case` clause of a `switch` statement, and we'll hold that in an inner function called `nextState(..)` that `next(..)` can call. Also, because `x` is a variable across the overall scope of the "generator," it needs to live outside the `nextState(..)` function.

Here it is all together (obviously somewhat simplified, to keep the conceptual illustration clearer):

```
function foo() {
    function nextState(v) {
        switch (state) {
            case 0:
                state++;

                // the `yield` expression
                return 42;
            case 1:
                state++;

                // `yield` expression fulfilled
                x = v;
                console.log( x );

                // the implicit `return`
                return undefined;

            // no need to handle state `2`
```

```
        }
    }

    var state = 0, x;

    return {
        next: function(v) {
            var ret = nextState( v );

            return { value: ret, done: (state == 2) };
        }

        // we'll skip `return(..)` and `throw(..)`
    };
}
```

And finally, let's test our pre-ES6 "generator":

```
var it = foo();

it.next();              // { value: 42, done: false }

it.next( 10 );          // 10
                        // { value: undefined, done: true }
```

Not bad, huh? Hopefully this exercise solidifies in your mind that generators are actually just simple syntax for state machine logic. That makes them widely applicable.

Generator Uses

So, now that we much more deeply understand how generators work, what are they useful for?

We've seen two major patterns:

Producing a series of values
> This usage can be simple (e.g., random strings or incremented numbers), or it can represent more structured data access (e.g., iterating over rows returned from a database query).

> Either way, we use the iterator to control a generator so that some logic can be invoked for each call to next(..). Normal iterators on data structures merely pull values without any controlling logic.

Queue of tasks to perform serially
> This usage often represents flow control for the steps in an algorithm, where each step requires retrieval of data from some

external source. The fulfillment of each piece of data may be immediate, or may be asynchronously delayed.

From the perspective of the code inside the generator, the details of sync or async at a `yield` point are entirely opaque. Moreover, these details are intentionally abstracted away, such as not to obscure the natural sequential expression of steps with such implementation complications. Abstraction also means the implementations can be swapped/refactored often without touching the code in the generator at all.

When generators are viewed in light of these uses, they become a lot more than just a different or nicer syntax for a manual state machine. They are a powerful abstraction tool for organizing and controlling orderly production and consumption of data.

Modules

I don't think it's an exaggeration to suggest that the single most important code organization pattern in all of JavaScript is, and always has been, the module. For myself, and I think for a large cross-section of the community, the module pattern drives the vast majority of code.

The Old Way

The traditional module pattern is based on an outer function with inner variables and functions, and a returned "public API" with methods that have closure over the inner data and capabilities. It's often expressed like this:

```
function Hello(name) {
    function greeting() {
        console.log( "Hello " + name + "!" );
    }

    // public API
    return {
        greeting: greeting
    };
}

var me = Hello( "Kyle" );
me.greeting();          // Hello Kyle!
```

This `Hello(..)` module can produce multiple instances by being called subsequent times. Sometimes, a module is only called for as a singleton (i.e., it just needs one instance), in which case a slight variation on the previous snippet, using an IIFE, is common:

```
var me = (function Hello(name){
    function greeting() {
        console.log( "Hello " + name + "!" );
    }

    // public API
    return {
        greeting: greeting
    };
})( "Kyle" );

me.greeting();          // Hello Kyle!
```

This pattern is tried and tested. It's also flexible enough to have a wide assortment of variations for a number of different scenarios.

One of the most common is the Asynchronous Module Definition (AMD), and another is the Universal Module Definition (UMD). We won't cover the particulars of these patterns and techniques here, but they're explained extensively in many places online.

Moving Forward

As of ES6, we no longer need to rely on the enclosing function and closure to provide us with module support. ES6 modules have first class syntactic and functional support.

Before we get into the specific syntax, it's important to understand some fairly significant conceptual differences with ES6 modules compared to how you may have dealt with modules in the past:

- ES6 uses file-based modules, meaning one module per file. At this time, there is no standardized way of combining multiple modules into a single file.

  That means that if you are going to load ES6 modules directly into a browser web application, you will be loading them individually, not as a large bundle in a single file as has been common in performance optimization efforts.

  It's expected that the contemporaneous advent of HTTP/2 will significantly mitigate any such performance concerns, as it operates on a persistent socket connection and thus can very efficiently load many smaller files in parallel and interleaved with one another.

- The API of an ES6 module is static. That is, you define statically what all the top-level exports are on your module's public API, and those cannot be amended later.

  Some uses are accustomed to being able to provide dynamic API definitions, where methods can be added/removed/replaced in response to runtime conditions. Either these uses will have to change to fit with ES6 static APIs, or they will have to restrain the dynamic changes to properties/methods of a second-level object.

- ES6 modules are singletons. That is, there's only one instance of the module, which maintains its state. Every time you import that module into another module, you get a reference to the one centralized instance. If you want to be able to produce multiple module instances, your module will need to provide some sort of factory to do it.

- The properties and methods you expose on a module's public API are not just normal assignments of values or references. They are actual bindings (almost like pointers) to the identifiers in your inner module definition.

  In pre-ES6 modules, if you put a property on your public API that holds a primitive value like a number or string, that property assignment was by value-copy, and any internal update of a corresponding variable would be separate and not affect the public copy on the API object.

  With ES6, exporting a local private variable, even if it currently holds a primitive string/number/etc., exports a binding to the variable. If the module changes the variable's value, the external import binding now resolves to that new value.

- Importing a module is the same thing as statically requesting it to load (if it hasn't already). If you're in a browser, that implies a blocking load over the network. If you're on a server (i.e., Node.js), it's a blocking load from the filesystem.

  However, don't panic about the performance implications. Because ES6 modules have static definitions, the import requirements can be statically scanned, and loads will happen preemptively, even before you've used the module.

ES6 doesn't actually specify or handle the mechanics of how these load requests work. There's a separate notion of a Module Loader, where each hosting environment (browser, Node.js, etc.) provides a default Loader appropriate to the environment. The importing of a module uses a string value to represent where to get the module (URL, file path, etc.), but this value is opaque in your program and only meaningful to the Loader itself.

You can define your own custom Loader if you want more fine-grained control than the default Loader affords—which is basically none, as it's totally hidden from your program's code.

As you can see, ES6 modules will serve the overall use case of organizing code with encapsulation, controlling public APIs, and referencing dependency imports. But they have a very particular way of doing so, and that may or may not fit very closely with how you've already been doing modules for years.

CommonJS

There's a similar, but not fully compatible, module syntax called CommonJS, which is familiar to those in the Node.js ecosystem.

For lack of a more tactful way to say this, in the long run, ES6 modules essentially are bound to supercede all previous formats and standards for modules, even CommonJS, as they are built on syntactic support in the language. This will, in time, inevitably win out as the superior approach, if for no other reason than ubiquity.

We face a fairly long road to get to that point, though. There are literally hundreds of thousands of CommonJS style modules in the server-side JavaScript world, and 10 times that many modules of varying format standards (UMD, AMD, ad hoc) in the browser world. It will take many years for the transitions to make any significant progress.

In the interim, module transpilers/converters will be an absolute necessity. You might as well just get used to that new reality. Whether you author in regular modules, AMD, UMD, CommonJS, or ES6, these tools will have to parse and convert to a format that is suitable for whatever environment your code will run in.

For Node.js, that probably means (for now) that the target is CommonJS. For the browser, it's probably UMD or AMD. Expect lots of flux on this over the next few years as these tools mature and best practices emerge.

From here on out, my best advice on modules is this: whatever format you've been religiously attached to with strong affinity, also develop an appreciation for and understanding of ES6 modules, such as they are, and let your other module tendencies fade. They *are* the future of modules in JS, even if that reality is a bit of a ways off.

The New Way

The two main new keywords that enable ES6 modules are import and export. There's lots of nuance to the syntax, so let's take a deeper look.

 An important detail that's easy to overlook: both import and export must always appear in the top-level scope of their respective usage. For example, you cannot put either an import or export inside an if conditional; they must appear outside of all blocks and functions.

Exporting API Members

The export keyword is either put in front of a declaration, or used as an operator (of sorts) with a special list of bindings to export. Consider:

```
export function foo() {
    // ..
}

export var awesome = 42;

var bar = [1,2,3];
export { bar };
```

Another way of expressing the same exports:

```
function foo() {
    // ..
}

var awesome = 42;
var bar = [1,2,3];
```

```
export { foo, awesome, bar };
```

These are all called *named exports*, as you are in effect exporting the name bindings of the variables/functions/etc.

Anything you don't *label* with `export` stays private inside the scope of the module. That is, although something like `var bar = ..` looks like it's declaring at the top-level global scope, the top-level scope is actually the module itself; there is no global scope in modules.

 Modules *do* still have access to `window` and all the "globals" that hang off it, just not as lexical top-level scope. However, you really should stay away from the globals in your modules if at all possible.

You can also "rename" (aka alias) a module member during named export:

```
function foo() { .. }

export { foo as bar };
```

When this module is imported, only the `bar` member name is available to import; `foo` stays hidden inside the module.

Module exports are not just normal assignments of values or references, as you're accustomed to with the = assignment operator. Actually, when you export something, you're exporting a binding (kinda like a pointer) to that thing (variable, etc.).

Within your module, if you change the value of a variable you already exported a binding to, even if it's already been imported (see the next section), the imported binding will resolve to the current (updated) value.

Consider:

```
var awesome = 42;
export { awesome };

// later
awesome = 100;
```

When this module is imported, regardless of whether that's before or after the `awesome` = `100` setting, once that assignment has happened, the imported binding resolves to the `100` value, not `42`.

That's because the binding is, in essence, a reference to, or a pointer to, the `awesome` variable itself, rather than a copy of its value. This is a mostly unprecedented concept for JS introduced with ES6 module bindings.

Though you can clearly use `export` multiple times inside a module's definition, ES6 definitely prefers the approach that a module has a single export, which is known as a *default export*. In the words of some members of the TC39 committee, you're "rewarded with simpler `import` syntax" if you follow that pattern, and conversely "penalized" with more verbose syntax if you don't.

A default export sets a particular exported binding to be the default when importing the module. The name of the binding is literally `default`. As you'll see later, when importing module bindings you can also rename them, as you commonly will with a default export.

There can only be one `default` per module definition. We'll cover `import` in the next section, and you'll see how the `import` syntax is more concise if the module has a default export.

There's a subtle nuance to default export syntax that you should pay close attention to. Compare these two snippets:

```
function foo(..) {
    // ..
}

export default foo;
```

And this one:

```
function foo(..) {
    // ..
}

export { foo as default };
```

In the first snippet, you are exporting a binding to the function expression value at that moment, *not* to the identifier foo. In other words, `export default` .. takes an expression. If you later assign foo to a different value inside your module, the module import still reveals the function originally exported, not the new value.

By the way, the first snippet could also have been written as:

```
export default function foo(..) {
    // ..
}
```

 Although the `function foo..` part here is technically a function expression, for the purposes of the internal scope of the module, it's treated like a function declaration, in that the `foo` name is bound in the module's top-level scope (often called "hoisting"). The same is true for `export default class Foo`... However, while you *can* do `export var foo = ..`, you currently cannot do `export default var foo = ..` (or `let` or `const`), in a frustrating case of inconsistency. At the time of this writing, there's already discussion of adding that capability in soon, post-ES6, for consistency's sake.

Recall the second snippet again:

```
function foo(..) {
    // ..
}

export { foo as default };
```

In this version of the module export, the default export binding is actually to the `foo` identifier rather than its value, so you get the previously described binding behavior (i.e., if you later change foo's value, the value seen on the import side will also be updated).

Be very careful of this subtle gotcha in default export syntax, especially if your logic calls for export values to be updated. If you never plan to update a default export's value, `export default ..` is fine. If you do plan to update the value, you must use `export { .. as default }`. Either way, make sure to comment your code to explain your intent!

Because there can only be one `default` per module, you may be tempted to design your module with one default export of an object with all your API methods on it, such as:

```
export default {
    foo() { .. },
    bar() { .. },
    ..
};
```

That pattern seems to map closely to how a lot of developers have already structured their pre-ES6 modules, so it seems like a natural approach. Unfortunately, it has some downsides and is officially discouraged.

In particular, the JS engine cannot statically analyze the contents of a plain object, which means it cannot do some optimizations for static `import` performance. The advantage of having each member individually and explicitly exported is that the engine *can* do the static analysis and optimization.

If your API has more than one member already, it seems like these principles—one default export per module, and all API members as named exports—are in conflict, doesn't it? But you *can* have a single default export as well as other named exports; they are not mutually exclusive.

So, instead of this (discouraged) pattern:

```
export default function foo() { .. }

foo.bar = function() { .. };
foo.baz = function() { .. };
```

You can do:

```
export default function foo() { .. }

export function bar() { .. }
export function baz() { .. }
```

 In this previous snippet, I used the name foo for the function that default labels. That foo name, however, is ignored for the purposes of export—default is actually the exported name. When you import this default binding, you can give it whatever name you want, as you'll see in the next section.

Alternatively, some will prefer:

```
function foo() { .. }
function bar() { .. }
function baz() { .. }

export { foo as default, bar, baz, .. };
```

The effects of mixing default and named exports will be more clear when we cover import shortly. But essentially it means that the most concise default import form would only retrieve the foo() function. The user could additionally manually list bar and baz as named imports, if they want them.

You can probably imagine how tedious that's going to be for consumers of your module if you have lots of named export bindings. There is a wildcard import form where you import all of a module's exports within a single namespace object, but there's no way to wildcard import to top-level bindings.

Again, the ES6 module mechanism is intentionally designed to discourage modules with lots of exports; relatively speaking, it's desired that such approaches be a little more difficult, as a sort of social engineering to encourage simple module design in favor of large/complex module design.

I would probably recommend that you avoid mixing default export with named exports, especially if you have a large API and refactoring to separate modules isn't practical or desired. In that case, just use all named exports, and document that consumers of your module should probably use the import * as .. (namespace import, discussed in the next section) approach to bring the whole API in at once on a single namespace.

We mentioned this earlier, but let's come back to it in more detail. Other than the export default ... form that exports an expression value binding, all other export forms are exporting bindings to local identifiers. For those bindings, if you change the value of a variable inside a module after exporting, the external imported binding will access the updated value:

```
var foo = 42;
export { foo as default };

export var bar = "hello world";

foo = 10;
bar = "cool";
```

When you import this module, the `default` and `bar` exports will be bound to the local variables `foo` and `bar`, meaning they will reveal the updated `10` and `"cool"` values. The values at time of export are irrelevant. The values at time of import are irrelevant. The bindings are live links, so all that matters is what the current value is when you access the binding.

Two-way bindings are not allowed. If you import a `foo` from a module, and try to change the value of your imported `foo` variable, an error will be thrown! We'll revisit that in the next section.

You can also re-export another module's exports, such as:

```
export { foo, bar } from "baz";
export { foo as FOO, bar as BAR } from "baz";
export * from "baz";
```

Those forms are similar to just first importing from the `"baz"` module then listing its members explicitly for export from your module. However, in these forms, the members of the `"baz"` module are never imported to your module's local scope; they sort of pass through untouched.

Importing API Members

To import a module, unsurprisingly you use the `import` statement. Just as `export` has several nuanced variations, so does `import`, so spend plenty of time considering the following issues and experimenting with your options.

If you want to import certain specific named members of a module's API into your top-level scope, you use this syntax:

```
import { foo, bar, baz } from "foo";
```

The `{ .. }` syntax here may look like an object literal, or even an object destructuring syntax. However, its form is special just for modules, so be careful not to confuse it with other `{ .. }` patterns elsewhere.

The "foo" string is called a *module specifier*. Because the whole goal is statically analyzable syntax, the module specifier must be a string literal; it cannot be a variable holding the string value.

From the perspective of your ES6 code and the JS engine itself, the contents of this string literal are completely opaque and meaningless. The module loader will interpret this string as an instruction of where to find the desired module, either as a URL path or a local filesystem path.

The foo, bar, and baz identifiers listed must match named exports on the module's API (static analysis and error assertion apply). They are bound as top-level identifiers in your current scope:

```
import { foo } from "foo";

foo();
```

You can rename the bound identifiers imported, as:

```
import { foo as theFooFunc } from "foo";

theFooFunc();
```

If the module has just a default export that you want to import and bind to an identifier, you can opt to skip the { .. } surrounding syntax for that binding. The import in this preferred case gets the nicest and most concise of the import syntax forms:

```
import foo from "foo";

// or:
import { default as foo } from "foo";
```

As explained in the previous section, the default keyword in a module's export specifies a named export where the name is actually default, as is illustrated by the second more verbose syntax option. The renaming from default to, in this case, foo, is explicit in the latter syntax and is identical yet implicit in the former syntax.

You can also import a default export along with other named exports, if the module has such a definition. Recall this module definition from earlier:

```
export default function foo() { .. }

export function bar() { .. }
export function baz() { .. }
```

To import that module's default export and its two named exports:

```
import FOOFN, { bar, baz as BAZ } from "foo";

FOOFN();
bar();
BAZ();
```

The strongly suggested approach from ES6's module philosophy is that you only import the specific bindings from a module that you need. If a module provides 10 API methods, but you only need two of them, some believe it wasteful to bring in the entire set of API bindings.

One benefit, besides code being more explicit, is that narrow imports make static analysis and error detection (accidentally using the wrong binding name, for instance) more robust.

Of course, that's just the standard position influenced by ES6 design philosophy; there's nothing that requires adherence to that approach.

Many developers would be quick to point out that such approaches can be more tedious, requiring you to regularly revisit and update your import statement(s) each time you realize you need something else from a module. The trade-off is in exchange for convenience.

In that light, the preference might be to import everything from the module into a single namespace, rather than importing individual members, each directly into the scope. Fortunately, the import statement has a syntax variation that can support this style of module consumption, called *namespace import*.

Consider a "foo" module exported as:

```
export function bar() { .. }
export var x = 42;
export function baz() { .. }
```

You can import that entire API to a single module namespace binding:

```
import * as foo from "foo";

foo.bar();
```

```
foo.x;          // 42
foo.baz();
```

 The * as .. clause requires the * wildcard. In other words, you cannot do something like import { bar, x } as foo from "foo" to bring in only part of the API but still bind to the foo namespace. I would have liked something like that, but for ES6 it's all or nothing with the namespace import.

If the module you're importing with * as .. has a default export, it is named default in the namespace specified. You can additionally name the default import outside of the namespace binding, as a top-level identifier. Consider a "world" module exported as:

```
export default function foo() { .. }
export function bar() { .. }
export function baz() { .. }
```

And this import:

```
import foofn, * as hello from "world";

foofn();
hello.default();
hello.bar();
hello.baz();
```

While this syntax is valid, it can be rather confusing that one method of the module (the default export) is bound at the top-level of your scope, whereas the rest of the named exports (and one called default) are bound as properties on a differently named (hello) identifier namespace.

As I mentioned earlier, my suggestion would be to avoid designing your module exports in this way, to reduce the chances that your module's users will suffer these strange quirks.

All imported bindings are immutable and/or read-only. Consider the previous import; all of these subsequent assignment attempts will throw TypeErrors:

```
import foofn, * as hello from "world";

foofn = 42;          // (runtime) TypeError!
hello.default = 42;  // (runtime) TypeError!
```

```
hello.bar = 42;      // (runtime) TypeError!
hello.baz = 42;      // (runtime) TypeError!
```

Recall earlier in "Exporting API Members" on page 120 that we talked about how the bar and baz bindings are bound to the actual identifiers inside the "world" module. That means if the module changes those values, hello.bar and hello.baz now reference the updated values.

But the immutable/read-only nature of your local imported bindings enforces that you cannot change them from the imported bindings, hence the TypeErrors. That's pretty important, because without those protections, your changes would end up affecting all other consumers of the module (remember: singleton), which could create some very surprising side effects!

Moreover, though a module *can* change its API members from the inside, you should be very cautious of intentionally designing your modules in that fashion. ES6 modules are *intended* to be static, so deviations from that principle should be rare and should be carefully and verbosely documented.

 There are module design philosophies where you actually intend to let a consumer change the value of a property on your API, or module APIs designed to be "extended" by having other "plug-ins" added to the API namespace. As we just asserted, ES6 module APIs should be thought of and designed as static and unchangeable, which strongly restricts and discourages these alternative module design patterns. You can get around these limitations by exporting a plain object, which of course can then be changed at will. But be careful and think twice before going down that road.

Declarations that occur as a result of an import are "hoisted" (see the *Scope & Closures* title of this series). Consider:

```
foo();

import { foo } from "foo";
```

foo() can run because not only did the static resolution of the import .. statement figure out what foo is during compilation, but it also "hoisted" the declaration to the top of the module's scope, thus making it available throughout the module.

Finally, the most basic form of the import looks like this:

```
import "foo";
```

This form does not actually import any of the module's bindings into your scope. It loads (if not already loaded), compiles (if not already compiled), and evaluates (if not already run) the "foo" module.

In general, that sort of import is probably not going to be terribly useful. There may be niche cases where a module's definition has side effects (such as assigning things to the window/global object). You could also envision using import "foo" as a sort of preload for a module that may be needed later.

Circular Module Dependency

A imports B. B imports A. How does this actually work?

I'll state off the bat that designing systems with intentional circular dependency is generally something I try to avoid. That having been said, I recognize there are reasons people do this and it can solve some sticky design situations.

Let's consider how ES6 handles this. First, module "A":

```
import bar from "B";

export default function foo(x) {
    if (x > 10) return bar( x - 1 );
    return x * 2;
}
```

Now, module "B":

```
import foo from "A";

export default function bar(y) {
    if (y > 5) return foo( y / 2 );
    return y * 3;
}
```

These two functions, foo(..) and bar(..), would work as standard function declarations if they were in the same scope, because the declarations are "hoisted" to the whole scope and thus available to each other regardless of authoring order.

With modules, you have declarations in entirely different scopes, so ES6 has to do extra work to help make these circular references work.

In a rough conceptual sense, this is how circular import dependencies are validated and resolved:

- If the "A" module is loaded first, the first step is to scan the file and analyze all the exports, so it can register all those bindings available for import. Then it processes the import .. from "B", which signals that it needs to go fetch "B".

- Once the engine loads "B", it does the same analysis of its export bindings. When it sees the import .. from "A", it knows the API of "A" already, so it can verify the import is valid. Now that it knows the "B" API, it can also validate the import .. from "B" in the waiting "A" module.

In essence, the mutual imports, along with the static verification that's done to validate both import statements, virtually composes the two separate module scopes (via the bindings), such that foo(..) can call bar(..) and vice versa. This is symmetric to if they had originally been declared in the same scope.

Now let's try using the two modules together. First, we'll try foo(..):

```
import foo from "foo";
foo( 25 );              // 11
```

Or we can try bar(..):

```
import bar from "bar";
bar( 25 );              // 11.5
```

By the time either the foo(25) or bar(25) calls are executed, all the analysis/compilation of all modules has completed. That means foo(..) internally knows directly about bar(..) and bar(..) internally knows directly about foo(..).

If all we need is to interact with foo(..), then we only need to import the "foo" module. Likewise with bar(..) and the "bar" module.

Of course, we *can* import and use both of them if we want to:

```
import foo from "foo";
import bar from "bar";

foo( 25 );              // 11
bar( 25 );              // 11.5
```

The static loading semantics of the import statement mean a "foo" and "bar" that mutually depend on each other via import will ensure that both are loaded, parsed, and compiled before either of them runs. So their circular dependency is statically resolved and this works as you'd expect.

Module Loading

We asserted at the beginning of "Modules" on page 116 that the import statement uses a separate mechanism, provided by the hosting environment (browser, Node.js, etc.), to actually resolve the module specifier string into some useful instruction for finding and loading the desired module. That mechanism is the system *Module Loader*.

The default module loader provided by the environment will interpret a module specifier as a URL if in the browser, and (generally) as a local filesystem path if on a server such as Node.js. The default behavior is to assume the loaded file is authored in the ES6 standard module format.

Moreover, you will be able to load a module into the browser via an HTML tag, similar to how current script programs are loaded. At the time of this writing, it's not fully clear if this tag will be `<script type="module">` or `<module>`. ES6 doesn't control that decision, but discussions in the appropriate standards bodies are already well along in parallel of ES6.

Whatever the tag looks like, you can be sure that under the covers it will use the default loader (or a customized one you've prespecified, as we'll discuss in the next section).

Just like the tag you'll use in markup, the module loader itself is not specified by ES6. It is a separate, parallel standard (*http://whatwg.github.io/loader/*) controlled currently by the WHATWG browser standards group.

At the time of this writing, the following discussions reflect an early pass at the API design, and things are likely to change.

Loading Modules Outside of Modules

One use for interacting directly with the module loader is if a non-module needs to load a module. Consider:

```
// normal script loaded in browser via `<script>`,
// `import` is illegal here

Reflect.Loader.import( "foo" ) // returns a promise for `"foo"`
.then( function(foo){
    foo.bar();
} );
```

The `Reflect.Loader.import(..)` utility imports the entire module onto the named parameter (as a namespace), just like the `import * as foo ..` namespace import we discussed earlier.

> The `Reflect.Loader.import(..)` utility returns a promise that is fulfilled once the module is ready. To import multiple modules, you can compose promises from multiple `Reflect.Loader.import(..)` calls using `Promise.all([ .. ])`. For more information about Promises, see "Promises" on page 147 in Chapter 4.

You can also use `Reflect.Loader.import(..)` in a real module to dynamically/conditionally load a module, where `import` itself would not work. You might, for instance, choose to load a module containing a polyfill for some ES7+ feature if a feature test reveals it's not defined by the current engine.

For performance reasons, you'll want to avoid dynamic loading whenever possible, as it hampers the ability of the JS engine to fire off early fetches from its static analysis.

Customized Loading

Another use for directly interacting with the module loader is if you want to customize its behavior through configuration or even redefinition.

At the time of this writing, there's a polyfill for the module loader API being developed (*https://github.com/ModuleLoader/es6-module-loader*). While details are scarce and highly subject to change, we can explore what possibilities may eventually land.

The `Reflect.Loader.import(..)` call may support a second argument for specifying various options to customize the import/load task. For example:

```
Reflect.Loader.import( "foo", { address: "/path/to/foo.js" } )
.then( function(foo){
    // ..
} )
```

It's also expected that a customization will be provided (through some means) for hooking into the process of loading a module, where a translation/transpilation could occur after load but before the engine compiles the module.

For example, you could load something that's not already an ES6-compliant module format (e.g., CoffeeScript, TypeScript, CommonJS, AMD). Your translation step could then convert it to an ES6-compliant module for the engine to then process.

Classes

From nearly the beginning of JavaScript, syntax and development patterns have all strived (read: struggled) to put on a facade of supporting class-oriented development. With things like new and `instanceof` and a `.constructor` property, who couldn't help but be teased that JS had classes hidden somewhere inside its prototype system?

Of course, JS "classes" aren't nearly the same as classical classes. The differences are well documented, so I won't belabor that point any further here.

 To learn more about the patterns used in JS to fake "classes," and an alternative view of prototypes called "delegation," see the second half of the *this & Object Prototypes* title of this series.

class

Although JS's prototype mechanism doesn't work like traditional classes, that doesn't stop the strong tide of demand on the language to extend the syntactic sugar so that expressing "classes" looks more like real classes. Enter the ES6 class keyword and its associated mechanism.

This feature is the result of a highly contentious and drawn-out debate, and represents a smaller subset compromise from several strongly opposed views on how to approach JS classes. Most developers who want full classes in JS will find parts of the new syntax quite inviting, but will find important bits still missing. Don't worry, though. TC39 is already working on additional features to augment classes in the post-ES6 timeframe.

At the heart of the new ES6 class mechanism is the `class` keyword, which identifies a *block* where the contents define the members of a function's prototype. Consider:

```
class Foo {
    constructor(a,b) {
        this.x = a;
        this.y = b;
    }

    gimmeXY() {
        return this.x * this.y;
    }
}
```

Some things to note:

- `class Foo` implies creating a (special) function of the name `Foo`, much like you did pre-ES6.
- `constructor(..)` identifies the signature of that `Foo(..)` function, as well as its body contents.
- Class methods use the same "concise method" syntax available to object literals, as discussed in Chapter 2. This also includes the concise generator form as discussed earlier in this chapter, as well as the ES5 getter/setter syntax. However, class methods are non-enumerable whereas object methods are by default enumerable.
- Unlike object literals, there are no commas separating members in a `class` body! In fact, they're not even allowed.

The `class` syntax definition in the previous snippet can be roughly thought of as this pre-ES6 equivalent, which probably will look fairly familiar to those who've done prototype-style coding before:

```
function Foo(a,b) {
    this.x = a;
    this.y = b;
```

```
    }

    Foo.prototype.gimmeXY = function() {
        return this.x * this.y;
    }
```

In either the pre-ES6 form or the new ES6 `class` form, this "class" can now be instantiated and used just as you'd expect:

```
var f = new Foo( 5, 15 );

f.x;                    // 5
f.y;                    // 15
f.gimmeXY();            // 75
```

Caution! Though `class Foo` seems much like `function Foo()`, there are important differences:

- A `Foo(..)` call of `class Foo` *must* be made with `new`, as the pre-ES6 option of `Foo.call( obj )` will *not* work.

- While `function Foo` is "hoisted" (see the *Scope & Closures* title of this series), `class Foo` is not; the `extends ..` clause specifies an expression that cannot be "hoisted." So, you must declare a `class` before you can instantiate it.

- `class Foo` in the top global scope creates a lexical Foo identifier in that scope, but unlike `function Foo` does not create a global object property of that name.

The established `instanceof` operator still works with ES6 classes, because `class` just creates a constructor function of the same name. However, ES6 introduces a way to customize how `instanceof` works, using `Symbol.hasInstance` (see "Well-Known Symbols" on page 203 in Chapter 7).

Another way of thinking about `class`, which I find more convenient, is as a *macro* that is used to automatically populate a proto type object. Optionally, it also wires up the `[[Prototype]]` relationship if using `extends` (see the next section).

An ES6 `class` isn't really an entity itself, but a meta concept that wraps around other concrete entities, such as functions and properties, and ties them together.

In addition to the declaration form, a `class` can also be an expression, as in: `var x = class Y { .. }`. This is primarily useful for passing a class definition (technically, the constructor itself) as a function argument or assigning it to an object property.

extends and super

ES6 classes also have syntactic sugar for establishing the `[[Proto type]]` delegation link between two function prototypes—commonly mislabeled "inheritance" or confusingly labeled "prototype inheritance"—using the class-oriented familiar terminology `extends`:

```
class Bar extends Foo {
    constructor(a,b,c) {
        super( a, b );
        this.z = c;
    }

    gimmeXYZ() {
        return super.gimmeXY() * this.z;
    }
}

var b = new Bar( 5, 15, 25 );

b.x;                    // 5
b.y;                    // 15
b.z;                    // 25
b.gimmeXYZ();           // 1875
```

A significant new addition is `super`, which is actually something not directly possible pre-ES6 (without some unfortunate hack tradeoffs). In the constructor, `super` automatically refers to the "parent constructor," which in the previous example is `Foo(..)`. In a method, it refers to the "parent object," such that you can then make a property/method access off it, such as `super.gimmeXY()`.

`Bar extends Foo` of course means to link the `[[Prototype]]` of `Bar.prototype` to `Foo.prototype`. So, `super` in a method like `gim meXYZ()` specifically means `Foo.prototype`, whereas `super` means `Foo` when used in the `Bar` constructor.

---

super is not limited to class declarations. It also works in object literals, in much the same way we're discussing here. See "Object super" on page 47 in Chapter 2 for more information.

There Be super Dragons

It is not insignificant to note that super behaves differently depending on where it appears. In fairness, most of the time, that won't be a problem. But surprises await if you deviate from a narrow norm.

There may be cases where in the constructor you would want to reference the Foo.prototype, such as to directly access one of its properties/methods. However, super in the constructor cannot be used in that way; super.prototype will not work. super(..) means roughly to call new Foo(..), but isn't actually a usable reference to Foo itself.

Symmetrically, you may want to reference the Foo(..) function from inside a nonconstructor method. super.constructor will point at Foo(..) the function, but beware that this function can *only* be invoked with new. new super.constructor(..) would be valid, but it wouldn't be terribly useful in most cases, because you can't make that call use or reference the current this object context, which is likely what you'd want.

Also, super looks like it might be driven by a function's context just like this—that is, that they'd both be dynamically bound. However, super is not dynamic like this is. When a constructor or method makes a super reference inside it at declaration time (in the class body), that super is statically bound to that specific class hierarchy, and cannot be overridden (at least in ES6).

What does that mean? It means that if you're in the habit of taking a method from one "class" and "borrowing" it for another class by overriding its this, say with call(..) or apply(..), that may very well create surprises if the method you're borrowing has a super in it. Consider this class hierarchy:

```
class ParentA {
    constructor() { this.id = "a"; }
    foo() { console.log( "ParentA:", this.id ); }
}

class ParentB {
```

```
        constructor() { this.id = "b"; }
        foo() { console.log( "ParentB:", this.id ); }
    }

    class ChildA extends ParentA {
        foo() {
            super.foo();
            console.log( "ChildA:", this.id );
        }
    }

    class ChildB extends ParentB {
        foo() {
            super.foo();
            console.log( "ChildB:", this.id );
        }
    }

    var a = new ChildA();
    a.foo();                    // ParentA: a
                                // ChildA: a
    var b = new ChildB();       // ParentB: b
    b.foo();                    // ChildB: b
```

All seems fairly natural and expected in this previous snippet. However, if you try to borrow b.foo() and use it in the context of a—by virtue of dynamic this binding, such borrowing is quite common and used in many different ways, including mixins most notably—you may find this result an ugly surprise:

```
// borrow `b.foo()` to use in `a` context
b.foo.call( a );            // ParentB: a
                            // ChildB: a
```

As you can see, the this.id reference was dynamically rebound so that : a is reported in both cases instead of : b. But b.foo()'s super.foo() reference wasn't dynamically rebound, so it still reported ParentB instead of the expected ParentA.

Because b.foo() references super, it is statically bound to the ChildB/ParentB hierarchy and cannot be used against the ChildA/ParentA hierarchy. There is no ES6 solution to this limitation.

super seems to work intuitively if you have a static class hierarchy with no cross-pollination. But in all fairness, one of the main benefits of doing this-aware coding is exactly that sort of flexibility. Simply, class + super requires you to avoid such techniques.

The choice boils down to narrowing your object design to these static hierarchies—class, extends, and super will be quite nice—or dropping all attempts to "fake" classes and instead embrace dynamic and flexible, classless objects and [[Prototype]] delegation (see the *this & Object Prototypes* title of this series).

Subclass Constructor

Constructors are not required for classes or subclasses; a default constructor is substituted in both cases if omitted. However, the default substituted constructor is different for a direct class versus an extended class.

Specifically, the default subclass constructor automatically calls the parent constructor, and passes along any arguments. In other words, you could think of the default subclass constructor sort of like this:

```
constructor(...args) {
    super(...args);
}
```

This is an important detail to note. Not all class languages have the subclass constructor automatically call the parent constructor. C++ does, but Java does not. But more importantly, in pre-ES6 classes, such automatic "parent constructor" calling does not happen. Be careful when converting to the ES6 class if you've been relying on such calls *not* happening.

Another perhaps surprising deviation/limitation of ES6 subclass constructors: in a constructor of a subclass, you cannot access this until super(..) has been called. The reason is nuanced and complicated, but it boils down to the fact that the parent constructor is actually the one creating/initializing your instance's this. Pre-ES6, it works oppositely; the this object is created by the "subclass constructor," and then you call a "parent constructor" with the context of the "subclass" this.

Let's illustrate. This works pre-ES6:

```
function Foo() {
    this.a = 1;
}

function Bar() {
    this.b = 2;
    Foo.call( this );
}
```

```
// `Bar` "extends" `Foo`
Bar.prototype = Object.create( Foo.prototype );
```

But this ES6 equivalent is not allowed:

```
class Foo {
    constructor() { this.a = 1; }
}

class Bar extends Foo {
    constructor() {
        this.b = 2;          // not allowed before `super()`
        super();             // to fix swap these two statements
    }
}
```

In this case, the fix is simple. Just swap the two statements in the subclass Bar constructor. However, if you've been relying pre-ES6 on being able to skip calling the "parent constructor," beware because that won't be allowed anymore.

extending Natives

One of the most heralded benefits to the new class and extend design is the ability to (finally!) subclass the built-in natives, like Array. Consider:

```
class MyCoolArray extends Array {
    first() { return this[0]; }
    last() { return this[this.length - 1]; }
}

var a = new MyCoolArray( 1, 2, 3 );

a.length;                // 3
a;                       // [1,2,3]

a.first();               // 1
a.last();                // 3
```

Prior to ES6, a fake "subclass" of Array using manual object creation and linking to Array.prototype only partially worked. It missed out on the special behaviors of a real array, such as the automatically updating length property. ES6 subclasses should fully work with "inherited" and augmented behaviors as expected!

Another common pre-ES6 "subclass" limitation is with the Error object, in creating custom error "subclasses." When genuine Error objects are created, they automatically capture special `stack` information, including the line number and file where the error is created. Pre-ES6 custom error "subclasses" have no such special behavior, which severely limits their usefulness.

ES6 to the rescue:

```
class Oops extends Error {
    constructor(reason) {
        this.oops = reason;
    }
}

// later:
var ouch = new Oops( "I messed up!" );
throw ouch;
```

The ouch custom error object in this previous snippet will behave like any other genuine error object, including capturing `stack`. That's a big improvement!

new.target

ES6 introduces a new concept called a *meta property* (see Chapter 7), in the form of `new.target`.

If that looks strange, it is; pairing a keyword with a . and a property name is definitely an out-of-the-ordinary pattern for JS.

`new.target` is a new "magical" value available in all functions, though in normal functions it will always be `undefined`. In any constructor, `new.target` always points at the constructor that `new` actually directly invoked, even if the constructor is in a parent class and was delegated to by a `super(..)` call from a child constructor. Consider:

```
class Foo {
    constructor() {
        console.log( "Foo: ", new.target.name );
    }
}

class Bar extends Foo {
    constructor() {
        super();
        console.log( "Bar: ", new.target.name );
    }
    baz() {
        console.log( "baz: ", new.target );
```

```
        }
    }

    var a = new Foo();
    // Foo: Foo

    var b = new Bar();
    // Foo: Bar    <-- respects the `new` call-site
    // Bar: Bar

    b.baz();
    // baz: undefined
```

The new.target meta property doesn't have much purpose in class constructors, except accessing a static property/method (see the next section).

If new.target is undefined, you know the function was not called with new. You can then force a new invocation if that's necessary.

static

When a subclass Bar extends a parent class Foo, we already observed that Bar.prototype is [[Prototype]]-linked to Foo.prototype. But additionally, Bar() is [[Prototype]]-linked to Foo(). That part may not have such an obvious reasoning.

However, it's quite useful in the case where you declare static methods (not just properties) for a class, as these are added directly to that class's function object, not to the function object's prototype object. Consider:

```
    class Foo {
        static cool() { console.log( "cool" ); }
        wow() { console.log( "wow" ); }
    }

    class Bar extends Foo {
        static awesome() {
            super.cool();
            console.log( "awesome" );
        }
        neat() {
            super.wow();
            console.log( "neat" );
        }
    }

    Foo.cool();                 // "cool"
```

```
Bar.cool();                // "cool"
Bar.awesome();             // "cool"
                           // "awesome"

var b = new Bar();
b.neat();                  // "wow"
                           // "neat"

b.awesome;                 // undefined
b.cool;                    // undefined
```

Be careful not to get confused that `static` members are on the class's prototype chain. They're actually on the dual/parallel chain between the function constructors.

Symbol.species Constructor Getter

One place where `static` can be useful is in setting the `Symbol.spe cies` getter (known internally in the specification as `@@species`) for a derived (child) class. This capability allows a child class to signal to a parent class what constructor should be used—when not intending the child class's constructor itself—if any parent class method needs to vend a new instance.

For example, many methods on `Array` create and return a new `Array` instance. If you define a derived class from `Array`, but you want those methods to continue to vend actual `Array` instances instead of from your derived class, this works:

```
class MyCoolArray extends Array {
    // force `species` to be parent constructor
    static get [Symbol.species]() { return Array; }
}

var a = new MyCoolArray( 1, 2, 3 ),
    b = a.map( function(v){ return v * 2; } );

b instanceof MyCoolArray;   // false
b instanceof Array;         // true
```

To illustrate how a parent class method can use a child's species declaration somewhat like `Array#map(..)` is doing, consider:

```
class Foo {
    // defer `species` to derived constructor
    static get [Symbol.species]() { return this; }
    spawn() {
        return new this.constructor[Symbol.species]();
    }
```

```
    }

    class Bar extends Foo {
        // force `species` to be parent constructor
        static get [Symbol.species]() { return Foo; }
    }

    var a = new Foo();
    var b = a.spawn();
    b instanceof Foo;                   // true

    var x = new Bar();
    var y = x.spawn();
    y instanceof Bar;                   // false
    y instanceof Foo;                   // true
```

The parent class Symbol.species does return this to defer to any derived class, as you'd normally expect. Bar then overrides to manually declare Foo to be used for such instance creation. Of course, a derived class can still vend instances of itself using new this.con structor(..).

Review

ES6 introduces several new features that aid in code organization:

- Iterators provide sequential access to data or operations. They can be consumed by new language features like for..of and ....

- Generators are locally pause/resume capable functions controlled by an iterator. They can be used to programmatically (and interactively, through yield/next(..) message passing) *generate* values to be consumed via iteration.

- Modules allow private encapsulation of implementation details with a publicly exported API. Module definitions are file-based, singleton instances, and statically resolved at compile time.

- Classes provide cleaner syntax around prototype-based coding. The addition of super also solves tricky issues with relative references in the [[Prototype]] chain.

These new tools should be your first stop when trying to improve the architecture of your JS projects by embracing ES6.

CHAPTER 4

Async Flow Control

It's no secret if you've written any significant amount of JavaScript that asynchronous programming is a required skill. The primary mechanism for managing asynchrony has been the function callback.

However, ES6 adds a new feature that helps address significant shortcomings in the callbacks-only approach to async: *Promises*. In addition, we can revisit generators (from the previous chapter) and see a pattern for combining the two that's a major step forward in async flow control programming in JavaScript.

Promises

Let's clear up some misconceptions: Promises are not about replacing callbacks. Promises provide a trustable intermediary—that is, between your calling code and the async code that will perform the task—to manage callbacks.

Another way of thinking about a Promise is as an event listener, upon which you can register to listen for an event that lets you know when a task has completed. It's an event that will only ever fire once, but it can be thought of as an event nonetheless.

Promises can be chained together, which can sequence a series of asychronously completing steps. Together with higher-level abstractions like the all(..) method (in classic terms, a "gate") and the race(..) method (in classic terms, a "latch"), promise chains provide an approximation of async flow control.

Yet another way of conceptualizing a Promise is that it's a *future value*, a time-independent container wrapped around a value. This container can be reasoned about identically whether the underlying value is final or not. Observing the resolution of a Promise extracts this value once available. In other words, a Promise is said to be the async version of a sync function's return value.

A Promise can only have one of two possible resolution outcomes: fulfilled or rejected, with an optional single value. If a Promise is fulfilled, the final value is called a fulfillment. If it's rejected, the final value is called a reason (as in, a "reason for rejection"). Promises can only be resolved (fulfillment or rejection) *once*. Any further attempts to fulfill or reject are simply ignored. Thus, once a Promise is resolved, it's an immutable value that cannot be changed.

Clearly, there are several different ways to think about what a Promise is. No single perspective is fully sufficient, but each provides a separate aspect of the whole. The big takeaway is that they offer a significant improvement over callbacks-only async, namely that they provide order, predictability, and trustability.

Making and Using Promises

To construct a promise instance, use the `Promise(..)` constructor:

```
var p = new Promise( function(resolve,reject){
    // ..
} );
```

The two parameters provided to the `Promise(..)` constructor are functions, and are generally named `resolve(..)` and `reject(..)`, respectively. They are used as:

- If you call `reject(..)`, the promise is rejected, and if any value is passed to `reject(..)`, it is set as the reason for rejection.

- If you call `resolve(..)` with no value, or any nonpromise value, the promise is fulfilled.

- If you call `resolve(..)` and pass another promise, this promise simply adopts the state—whether immediate or eventual—of the passed promise (either fulfillment or rejection).

Here's how you'd typically use a promise to refactor a callback-reliant function call. If you start out with an `ajax(..)` utility that expects to be able to call an error-first style callback:

```
function ajax(url,cb) {
    // make request, eventually call `cb(..)`
}

// ..

ajax( "http://some.url.1", function handler(err,contents){
    if (err) {
        // handle ajax error
    }
    else {
        // handle `contents` success
    }
} );
```

You can convert it to:

```
function ajax(url) {
    return new Promise( function pr(resolve,reject){
        // make request, eventually call
        // either `resolve(..)` or `reject(..)`
    } );
}

// ..

ajax( "http://some.url.1" )
.then(
    function fulfilled(contents){
        // handle `contents` success
    },
    function rejected(reason){
        // handle ajax error reason
    }
);
```

Promises have a then(..) method that accepts one or two callback functions. The first function (if present) is treated as the handler to call if the promise is fulfilled successfully. The second function (if present) is treated as the handler to call if the promise is rejected explicitly, or if any error/exception is caught during resolution.

If one of the arguments is omitted or otherwise not a valid function —typically you'll use null instead—a default placeholder equivalent is used. The default success callback passes its fulfillment value along and the default error callback propagates its rejection reason along.

The shorthand for calling then(null,handleRejection) is catch(handleRejection).

Both then(..) and catch(..) automatically construct and return another promise instance, which is wired to receive the resolution from whatever the return value is from the original promise's fulfillment or rejection handler (whichever is actually called). Consider:

```
ajax( "http://some.url.1" )
.then(
    function fulfilled(contents){
        return contents.toUpperCase();
    },
    function rejected(reason){
        return "DEFAULT VALUE";
    }
)
.then( function fulfilled(data){
    // handle data from original promise's
    // handlers
} );
```

In this snippet, we're returning an immediate value from either ful filled(..) or rejected(..), which then is received on the next event turn in the second then(..)'s fulfilled(..). If we instead return a new promise, that new promise is subsumed and adopted as the resolution:

```
ajax( "http://some.url.1" )
.then(
    function fulfilled(contents){
        return ajax(
            "http://some.url.2?v=" + contents
        );
    },
    function rejected(reason){
        return ajax(
            "http://backup.url.3?err=" + reason
        );
    }
)
.then( function fulfilled(contents){
    // `contents` comes from the subsequent
    // `ajax(..)` call, whichever it was
} );
```

It's important to note that an exception (or rejected promise) in the first fulfilled(..) will *not* result in the first rejected(..) being called, as that handler only responds to the resolution of the first original promise. Instead, the second promise, which the second then(..) is called against, receives that rejection.

In this previous snippet, we are not listening for that rejection, which means it will be silently held onto for future observation. If you never observe it by calling a then(..) or catch(..), then it will go unhandled. Some browser developer consoles may detect these unhandled rejections and report them, but this is not reliably guaranteed; you should always observe promise rejections.

> This was just a brief overview of Promise theory and behavior. For a much more in-depth exploration, see Chapter 3 of the *Async & Performance* title of this series.

Thenables

Promises are genuine instances of the Promise(..) constructor. However, there are promise-like objects called *thenables* that generally can interoperate with the Promise mechanisms.

Any object (or function) with a then(..) function on it is assumed to be a thenable. Any place where the Promise mechanisms can accept and adopt the state of a genuine promise, they can also handle a thenable.

Thenables are basically a general label for any promise-like value that may have been created by some other system than the actual Promise(..) constructor. In that perspective, a thenable is generally less trustable than a genuine Promise. Consider this misbehaving thenable, for example:

```
var th = {
    then: function thener( fulfilled ) {
        // call `fulfilled(..)` once every 100ms forever
        setInterval( fulfilled, 100 );
    }
};
```

If you received that thenable and chained it with th.then(..), you'd likely be surprised that your fulfillment handler is called repeatedly, when normal Promises are supposed to only ever be resolved once.

Generally, if you're receiving what purports to be a promise or thenable back from some other system, you shouldn't just trust it blindly. In the next section, we'll see a utility included with ES6 Promises that helps address this trust concern.

But to further understand the perils of this issue, consider that *any* object in *any* piece of code that's ever been defined to have a method on it called then(..) can be potentially confused as a thenable—if used with Promises, of course—regardless of if that thing was ever intended to even remotely be related to Promise-style async coding.

Prior to ES6, there was never any special reservation made on methods called then(..), and as you can imagine there's been at least a few cases where that method name has been chosen prior to Promises ever showing up on the radar screen. The most likely case of mistaken thenable will be async libraries that use then(..) but which are not strictly Promises-compliant—there are several out in the wild.

The onus will be on you to guard against directly using values with the Promise mechanism that would be incorrectly assumed to be a thenable.

Promise API

The Promise API also provides some static methods for working with Promises.

Promise.resolve(..) creates a promise resolved to the value passed in. Let's compare how it works to the more manual approach:

```
var p1 = Promise.resolve( 42 );

var p2 = new Promise( function pr(resolve){
    resolve( 42 );
} );
```

p1 and p2 will have essentially identical behavior. The same goes for resolving with a promise:

```
var theP = ajax( .. );

var p1 = Promise.resolve( theP );

var p2 = new Promise( function pr(resolve){
    resolve( theP );
} );
```

`Promise.resolve(..)` is the solution to the thenable trust issue raised in the previous section. Any value that you are not already certain is a trustable promise—even if it could be an immediate value—can be normalized by passing it to `Promise.resolve(..)`. If the value is already a recognizable promise or thenable, its state/resolution will simply be adopted, insulating you from misbehavior. If it's instead an immediate value, it will be "wrapped" in a genuine promise, thereby normalizing its behavior to be async.

`Promise.reject(..)` creates an immediately rejected promise, the same as its `Promise(..)` constructor counterpart:

```
var p1 = Promise.reject( "Oops" );

var p2 = new Promise( function pr(resolve,reject){
    reject( "Oops" );
} );
```

While `resolve(..)` and `Promise.resolve(..)` can accept a promise and adopt its state/resolution, `reject(..)` and `Promise.reject(..)` do not differentiate what value they receive. So, if you reject with a promise or thenable, the promise/thenable itself will be set as the rejection reason, not its underlying value.

`Promise.all([ .. ])` accepts an array of one or more values (e.g., immediate values, promises, thenables). It returns a promise back that will be fulfilled if all the values fulfill, or reject immediately once the first of any of them rejects.

Starting with these values/promises:

```
var p1 = Promise.resolve( 42 );
var p2 = new Promise( function pr(resolve){
    setTimeout( function(){
        resolve( 43 );
    }, 100 );
} );
var v3 = 44;
var p4 = new Promise( function pr(resolve,reject){
    setTimeout( function(){
        reject( "Oops" );
    }, 10 );
} );
```

Let's consider how `Promise.all([ .. ])` works with combinations of those values:

```
Promise.all( [p1,p2,v3] )
.then( function fulfilled(vals){
    console.log( vals );            // [42,43,44]
} );

Promise.all( [p1,p2,v3,p4] )
.then(
    function fulfilled(vals){
        // never gets here
    },
    function rejected(reason){
        console.log( reason );      // Oops
    }
);
```

While `Promise.all([ .. ])` waits for all fulfillments (or the first rejection), `Promise.race([ .. ])` waits only for either the first fulfillment or rejection. Consider:

```
// NOTE: re-setup all test values to
// avoid timing issues misleading you!

Promise.race( [p2,p1,v3] )
.then( function fulfilled(val){
    console.log( val );            // 42
} );

Promise.race( [p2,p4] )
.then(
    function fulfilled(val){
        // never gets here
    },
    function rejected(reason){
        console.log( reason );      // Oops
    }
);
```

While `Promise.all([])` will fulfill right away (with no values), `Promise.race([])` will hang forever. This is a strange inconsistency, and speaks to the suggestion that you should never use these methods with empty arrays.

Generators + Promises

It *is* possible to express a series of promises in a chain to represent the async flow control of your program. Consider:

```
step1()
.then(
    step2,
    step2Failed
)
.then(
    function(msg) {
        return Promise.all( [
            step3a( msg ),
            step3b( msg ),
            step3c( msg )
        ] )
    }
)
.then(step4);
```

However, there's a much better option for expressing async flow control, and it will probably be much more preferable in terms of coding style than long promise chains. We can use what we learned in Chapter 3 about generators to express our async flow control.

The important pattern to recognize: a generator can yield a promise, and that promise can then be wired to resume the generator with its fulfillment value.

Consider the previous snippet's async flow control expressed with a generator:

```
function *main() {
    var ret = yield step1();

    try {
        ret = yield step2( ret );
    }
    catch (err) {
        ret = yield step2Failed( err );
    }

    ret = yield Promise.all( [
        step3a( ret ),
        step3b( ret ),
        step3c( ret )
    ] );
```

```
        yield step4( ret );
    }
```

On the surface, this snippet may seem more verbose than the promise chain equivalent in the earlier snippet. However, it offers a much more attractive—and more importantly, a more understandable and reason-able—synchronous-looking coding style (with = assignment of "return" values, etc.) That's especially true in that `try..catch` error handling can be used across those hidden async boundaries.

Why are we using Promises with the generator? It's certainly possible to do async generator coding without Promises.

Promises are a trustable system that uninverts the inversion of control of normal callbacks or thunks (see the *Async & Performance* title of this series). So, combining the trustability of Promises and the synchronicity of code in generators effectively addresses all the major deficiencies of callbacks. Also, utilities like `Promise.all([ .. ])` are a nice, clean way to express concurrency at a generator's single `yield` step.

So how does this magic work? We're going to need a *runner* that can run our generator, receive a `yielded` promise, and wire it up to resume the generator with either the fulfillment success value, or throw an error into the generator with the rejection reason.

Many async-capable utilities/libraries have such a "runner"; for example, `Q.spawn(..)` and my asynquence's `runner(..)` plug-in. But here's a stand-alone runner to illustrate how the process works:

```
function run(gen) {
    var args = [].slice.call( arguments, 1), it;

    it = gen.apply( this, args );

    return Promise.resolve()
        .then( function handleNext(value){
            var next = it.next( value );

            return (function handleResult(next){
                if (next.done) {
                    return next.value;
                }
                else {
                    return Promise.resolve( next.value )
                        .then(
                            handleNext,
```

```
                function handleErr(err) {
                    return Promise.resolve(
                        it.throw( err )
                    )
                    .then( handleResult );
                }
            );
        }
    })( next );
} );
}
```

 For a more prolifically commented version of this utility, see the *Async & Performance* title of this series. Also, the run utilities provided with various async libraries are often more powerful/ capable than what we've shown here. For example, asynquence's `runner(..)` can handle `yielded` promises, sequences, thunks, and immediate (nonpromise) values, giving you ultimate flexibility.

So now running `*main()` as listed in the earlier snippet is as easy as:

```
run( main )
.then(
    function fulfilled(){
        // `*main()` completed successfully
    },
    function rejected(reason){
        // Oops, something went wrong
    }
);
```

Essentially, anywhere that you have more than two asynchronous steps of flow control logic in your program, you can *and should* use a promise-yielding generator driven by a run utility to express the flow control in a synchronous fashion. This will make for much easier to understand and maintain code.

This yield-a-promise-resume-the-generator pattern is going to be so common and so powerful, the next version of JavaScript is almost certainly going to introduce a new function type that will do it automatically without needing the run utility. We'll cover `async func tions` (as they're expected to be called) in Chapter 8.

Review

As JavaScript continues to mature and grow in its widespread adoption, asynchronous programming is more and more of a central concern. Callbacks are not fully sufficient for these tasks, and totally fall down the more sophisticated the need.

Thankfully, ES6 adds Promises to address one of the major shortcomings of callbacks: lack of trust in predictable behavior. Promises represent the future completion value from a potentially async task, normalizing behavior across sync and async boundaries.

But it's the combination of Promises with generators that fully realizes the benefits of rearranging our async flow control code to de-emphasize and abstract away that ugly callback soup (aka "hell").

Right now, we can manage these interactions with the aide of various async libraries' runners, but JavaScript is eventually going to support this interaction pattern with dedicated syntax alone!

CHAPTER 5

Collections

Structured collection and access to data is a critical component of just about any JS program. From the beginning of the language up to this point, the array and the object have been our primary mechanism for creating data structures. Of course, many higher-level data structures have been built on top of these, as user-land libraries.

As of ES6, some of the most useful (and performance-optimizing!) data structure abstractions have been added as native components of the language.

We'll start this chapter first by looking at *TypedArrays*, which were technically contemporary to ES5 efforts several years ago, but only standardized as companions to WebGL and not JavaScript itself. As of ES6, these have been adopted directly by the language specification, which gives them first-class status.

Maps are like objects (key/value pairs), but instead of just a string for the key, you can use any value—even another object or map! Sets are similar to arrays (lists of values), but the values are unique; if you add a duplicate, it's ignored. There are also weak (in relation to memory/garbage collection) counterparts: WeakMap and WeakSet.

TypedArrays

As we cover in the *Types & Grammar* title of this series, JS does have a set of built-in types, like number and string. It'd be tempting to look at a feature named "typed array" and assume it means an array of a specific type of values, like an array of only strings.

However, typed arrays are really more about providing structured access to binary data using array-like semantics (indexed access, etc.). The "type" in the name refers to a "view" layered on type of the bucket of bits, which is essentially a mapping of whether the bits should be viewed as an array of 8-bit signed integers, 16-bit signed integers, and so on.

How do you construct such a bit-bucket? It's called a "buffer," and you construct it most directly with the `ArrayBuffer(..)` constructor:

```
var buf = new ArrayBuffer( 32 );
buf.byteLength;                         // 32
```

buf is now a binary buffer that is 32-bytes long (256-bits), that's pre-initialized to all `0`s. A buffer by itself doesn't really allow you any interaction exception for checking its `byteLength` property.

 Several web platform features use or return array buffers, such as `FileReader#readAsArray Buffer(..)`, `XMLHttpRequest#send(..)`, and `ImageData` (canvas data).

But on top of this array buffer, you can then layer a "view," which comes in the form of a typed array. Consider:

```
var arr = new Uint16Array( buf );
arr.length;                     // 16
```

arr is a typed array of 16-bit unsigned integers mapped over the 256-bit buf buffer, meaning you get 16 elements.

Endianness

It's very important to understand that the arr is mapped using the endian-setting (big-endian or little-endian) of the platform the JS is running on. This can be an issue if the binary data is created with one endianness but interpreted on a platform with the opposite endianness.

Endian means if the low-order byte (collection of 8-bits) of a multi-byte number—such as the 16-bit unsigned ints we created in the earlier snippet—is on the right or the left of the number's bytes.

For example, let's imagine the base-10 number 3085, which takes 16-bits to represent. If you have just one 16-bit number container, it'd be represented in binary as 0000110000001101 (hexadecimal 0c0d) regardless of endianness.

But if 3085 was represented with two 8-bit numbers, the endianness would significantly affect its storage in memory:

- 0000110000001101 / 0c0d (big-endian)
- 0000110100001100 / 0d0c (little-endian)

If you received the bits of 3085 as 0000110100001100 from a little-endian system, but you layered a view on top of it in a big-endian system, you'd instead see value 3340 (base-10) and 0d0c (base-16).

Little-endian is the most common representation on the Web these days, but there are definitely browsers where that's not true. It's important that you understand the endianness of both the producer and consumer of a chunk of binary data.

From MDN, here's a quick way to test the endianness of your Java-Script:

```
var littleEndian = (function() {
    var buffer = new ArrayBuffer( 2 );
    new DataView( buffer ).setInt16( 0, 256, true );
    return new Int16Array( buffer )[0] === 256;
})();
```

littleEndian will be true or false; for most browsers, it should return true. This test uses DataView(..), which allows more low-level, fine-grained control over accessing (setting/getting) the bits from the view you layer over the buffer. The third parameter of the setInt16(..) method in the previous snippet is for telling the Data View what endianness you're wanting it to use for that operation.

Do not confuse endianness of underlying binary storage in array buffers with how a given number is represented when exposed in a JS program. For example, `(3085).toString(2)` returns `"110000001101"`, which with an assumed leading four `"0"`s appears to be the big-endian representation. In fact, this representation is based on a single 16-bit view, not a view of two 8-bit bytes. The `DataView` test above is the best way to determine endianness for your JS environment.

Multiple Views

A single buffer can have multiple views attached to it, such as:

```
var buf = new ArrayBuffer( 2 );

var view8 = new Uint8Array( buf );
var view16 = new Uint16Array( buf );

view16[0] = 3085;
view8[0];                       // 13
view8[1];                       // 12

view8[0].toString( 16 );        // "d"
view8[1].toString( 16 );        // "c"

// swap (as if endian!)
var tmp = view8[0];
view8[0] = view8[1];
view8[1] = tmp;

view16[0];                      // 3340
```

The typed array constructors have multiple signature variations. We've shown so far only passing them an existing buffer. However, that form also takes two extra parameters: `byteOffset` and `length`. In other words, you can start the typed array view at a location other than 0 and you can make it span less than the full length of the buffer.

If the buffer of binary data includes data in nonuniform size/location, this technique can be quite useful.

For example, consider a binary buffer that has a 2-byte number (aka "word") at the beginning, followed by two 1-byte numbers, followed by a 32-bit floating-point number. Here's how you can access that data with multiple views on the same buffer, offsets, and lengths:

```
var first = new Uint16Array( buf, 0, 2 )[0],
    second = new Uint8Array( buf, 2, 1 )[0],
    third = new Uint8Array( buf, 3, 1 )[0],
    fourth = new Float32Array( buf, 4, 4 )[0];
```

Typed Array Constructors

In addition to the (buffer,[offset, [length]]) form examined in the previous section, typed array constructors also support these forms:

- [constructor\](length): Creates a new view over a new buffer of length bytes
- [constructor\](typedArr): Creates a new view and buffer, and copies the contents from the typedArr view
- [constructor\](obj): Creates a new view and buffer, and iterates over the array-like or object obj to copy its contents

The following typed array constructors are available as of ES6:

- Int8Array (8-bit signed integers), Uint8Array (8-bit unsigned integers)
  - Uint8ClampedArray (8-bit unsigned integers, each value clamped on setting to the 0-255 range)
- Int16Array (16-bit signed integers), Uint16Array (16-bit unsigned integers)
- Int32Array (32-bit signed integers), Uint32Array (32-bit unsigned integers)
- Float32Array (32-bit floating point, IEEE-754)
- Float64Array (64-bit floating point, IEEE-754)

Instances of typed array constructors are almost the same as regular native arrays. Some differences include having a fixed length and the values all being of the same "type."

However, they share most of the same prototype methods. As such, you likely will be able to use them as regular arrays without needing to convert.

For example:

```
var a = new Int32Array( 3 );
a[0] = 10;
a[1] = 20;
a[2] = 30;

a.map( function(v){
    console.log( v );
} );
// 10 20 30

a.join( "-" );
// "10-20-30"
```

 You can't use certain `Array.prototype` methods with TypedArrays that don't make sense, such as the mutators (`splice(..)`, `push(..)`, etc.) and `concat(..)`.

Be aware that the elements in TypedArrays really are constrained to the declared bit sizes. If you have a `Uint8Array` and try to assign something larger than an 8-bit value into one of its elements, the value wraps around so as to stay within the bit length.

This could cause problems if you were trying to, for instance, square all the values in a TypedArray. Consider:

```
var a = new Uint8Array( 3 );
a[0] = 10;
a[1] = 20;
a[2] = 30;

var b = a.map( function(v){
    return v * v;
} );

b;                  // [100, 144, 132]
```

The 20 and 30 values, when squared, resulted in bit overflow. To get around such a limitation, you can use the `TypedArray#from(..)` function:

```
var a = new Uint8Array( 3 );
a[0] = 10;
a[1] = 20;
a[2] = 30;

var b = Uint16Array.from( a, function(v){
```

```
        return v * v;
    } );

    b;                      // [100, 400, 900]
```

See "Array.from(..) Static Function" on page 177 in Chapter 6 for more information about the `Array.from(..)` that is shared with TypedArrays. Specifically, "Mapping" on page 179 explains the mapping function accepted as its second argument.

One interesting behavior to consider is that TypedArrays have a `sort(..)` method much like regular arrays, but this one defaults to numeric sort comparisons instead of coercing values to strings for lexicographic comparison. For example:

```
var a = [ 10, 1, 2, ];
a.sort();                        // [1,10,2]

var b = new Uint8Array( [ 10, 1, 2 ] );
b.sort();                        // [1,2,10]
```

The `TypedArray#sort(..)` takes an optional compare function argument just like `Array#sort(..)`, which works in exactly the same way.

Maps

If you have a lot of JS experience, you know that objects are the primary mechanism for creating unordered key/value-pair data structures, otherwise known as maps. However, the major drawback with objects-as-maps is the inability to use a nonstring value as the key.

For example, consider:

```
var m = {};

var x = { id: 1 },
    y = { id: 2 };

m[x] = "foo";
m[y] = "bar";

m[x];                        // "bar"
m[y];                        // "bar"
```

What's going on here? The two objects x and y both stringify to `"[object Object]"`, so only that one key is being set in m.

Some have implemented fake maps by maintaining a parallel array of non-string keys alongside an array of the values, such as:

```
var keys = [], vals = [];

var x = { id: 1 },
    y = { id: 2 };

keys.push( x );
vals.push( "foo" );

keys.push( y );
vals.push( "bar" );

keys[0] === x;                  // true
vals[0];                        // "foo"

keys[1] === y;                  // true
vals[1];                        // "bar"
```

Of course, you wouldn't want to manage those parallel arrays yourself, so you could define a data structure with methods that automatically do the management under the covers. Besides having to do that work yourself, the main drawback is that access is no longer O(1) time-complexity, but instead is O(n).

But as of ES6, there's no longer any need to do this! Just use Map(..):

```
var m = new Map();

var x = { id: 1 },
    y = { id: 2 };

m.set( x, "foo" );
m.set( y, "bar" );

m.get( x );                     // "foo"
m.get( y );                     // "bar"
```

The only drawback is that you can't use the [ ] bracket access syntax for setting and retrieving values. But get(..) and set(..) work perfectly suitably instead.

To delete an element from a map, don't use the delete operator, but instead use the delete(..) method:

```
m.set( x, "foo" );
m.set( y, "bar" );

m.delete( y );
```

You can clear the entire map's contents with clear(). To get the length of a map (i.e., the number of keys), use the size property (not length):

```
m.set( x, "foo" );
m.set( y, "bar" );
m.size;                          // 2

m.clear();
m.size;                          // 0
```

The Map(..) constructor can also receive an iterable (see "Iterators" on page 87 in Chapter 3), which must produce a list of arrays, where the first item in each array is the key and the second item is the value. This format for iteration is identical to that produced by the entries() method, explained in the next section. That makes it easy to make a copy of a map:

```
var m2 = new Map( m.entries() );

// same as:
var m2 = new Map( m );
```

Because a map instance is an iterable, and its default iterator is the same as entries(), the second shorter form is preferable.

Of course, you can just manually specify an *entries* list (array of key/value arrays) in the Map(..) constructor form:

```
var x = { id: 1 },
    y = { id: 2 };

var m = new Map( [
    [ x, "foo" ],
    [ y, "bar" ]
] );

m.get( x );                      // "foo"
m.get( y );                      // "bar"
```

Map Values

To get the list of values from a map, use values(..), which returns an iterator. In Chapters 2 and 3, we covered various ways to process an iterator sequentially (like an array), such as the ... spread operator and the for..of loop. Also, "Creating Arrays and Subtypes" on page 179 in Chapter 6 covers the Array.from(..) method in detail. Consider:

```
var m = new Map();

var x = { id: 1 },
    y = { id: 2 };

m.set( x, "foo" );
m.set( y, "bar" );

var vals = [ ...m.values() ];

vals;                       // ["foo","bar"]
Array.from( m.values() );   // ["foo","bar"]
```

As discussed in the previous section, you can iterate over a map's entries using entries() (or the default map iterator). Consider:

```
var m = new Map();

var x = { id: 1 },
    y = { id: 2 };

m.set( x, "foo" );
m.set( y, "bar" );

var vals = [ ...m.entries() ];

vals[0][0] === x;           // true
vals[0][1];                 // "foo"

vals[1][0] === y;           // true
vals[1][1];                 // "bar"
```

Map Keys

To get the list of keys, use keys(), which returns an iterator over the keys in the map:

```
var m = new Map();

var x = { id: 1 },
    y = { id: 2 };

m.set( x, "foo" );
m.set( y, "bar" );

var keys = [ ...m.keys() ];

keys[0] === x;              // true
keys[1] === y;              // true
```

To determine if a map has a given key, use `has(..)`:

```
var m = new Map();

var x = { id: 1 },
    y = { id: 2 };

m.set( x, "foo" );

m.has( x );                    // true
m.has( y );                    // false
```

Maps essentially let you associate some extra piece of information (the value) with an object (the key) without actually putting that information on the object itself.

While you can use any kind of value as a key for a map, you typically will use objects, as strings and other primitives are already eligible as keys of normal objects. In other words, you'll probably want to continue to use normal objects for maps unless some or all of the keys need to be objects, in which case map is more appropriate.

 If you use an object as a map key and that object is later discarded (all references unset) in attempt to have garbage collection (GC) reclaim its memory, the map itself will still retain its entry. You will need to remove the entry from the map for it to be GC-eligible. In the next section, we'll see WeakMaps as a better option for object keys and GC.

WeakMaps

WeakMaps are a variation on maps, which has most of the same external behavior but differs underneath in how the memory allocation (specifically its GC) works.

WeakMaps take (only) objects as keys. Those objects are held *weakly*, which means if the object itself is GC'd, the entry in the WeakMap is also removed. This isn't observable behavior, though, as the only way an object can be GC'd is if there's no more references to it, but once there are no more references to it—you have no object reference to check if it exists in the WeakMap.

Otherwise, the API for WeakMap is similar, though more limited:

```
var m = new WeakMap();

var x = { id: 1 },
    y = { id: 2 };

m.set( x, "foo" );

m.has( x );                        // true
m.has( y );                        // false
```

WeakMaps do not have a size property or clear() method, nor do they expose any iterators over their keys, values, or entries. So even if you unset the x reference, which will remove its entry from m upon GC, there is no way to tell. You'll just have to take JavaScript's word for it!

Just like Maps, WeakMaps let you soft-associate information with an object. But they are particularly useful if the object is not one you completely control, such as a DOM element. If the object you're using as a map key can be deleted and should be GC-eligible when it is, then a WeakMap is a more appropriate option.

It's important to note that a WeakMap only holds its *keys* weakly, not its values. Consider:

```
var m = new WeakMap();

var x = { id: 1 },
    y = { id: 2 },
    z = { id: 3 },
    w = { id: 4 };

m.set( x, y );

x = null;             // { id: 1 } is GC-eligible
y = null;             // { id: 2 } is GC-eligible
                      // only because { id: 1 } is

m.set( z, w );

w = null;             // { id: 4 } is not GC-eligible
```

For this reason, WeakMaps are in my opinion better named "Weak-KeyMaps."

Sets

A set is a collection of unique values (duplicates are ignored).

The API for a set is similar to map. The add(..) method takes the place of the set(..) method (somewhat ironically), and there is no get(..) method.

Consider:

```
var s = new Set();

var x = { id: 1 },
    y = { id: 2 };

s.add( x );
s.add( y );
s.add( x );

s.size;                          // 2

s.delete( y );
s.size;                          // 1

s.clear();
s.size;                          // 0
```

The Set(..) constructor form is similar to Map(..), in that it can receive an iterable, like another set or simply an array of values. However, unlike how Map(..) expects an *entries* list (array of key/value arrays), Set(..) expects a *values* list (array of values):

```
var x = { id: 1 },
    y = { id: 2 };

var s = new Set( [x,y] );
```

A set doesn't need a get(..) because you don't retrieve a value from a set, but rather test if it is present or not, using has(..):

```
var s = new Set();

var x = { id: 1 },
    y = { id: 2 };

s.add( x );

s.has( x );                      // true
s.has( y );                      // false
```

The comparison algorithm in has(..) is almost identical to Object.is(..) (see Chapter 6), except that -0 and 0 are treated as the same rather than distinct.

Set Iterators

Sets have the same iterator methods as maps. Their behavior is different for sets, but symmetric with the behavior of map iterators. Consider:

```
var s = new Set();

var x = { id: 1 },
    y = { id: 2 };

s.add( x ).add( y );

var keys = [ ...s.keys() ],
    vals = [ ...s.values() ],
    entries = [ ...s.entries() ];

keys[0] === x;
keys[1] === y;

vals[0] === x;
vals[1] === y;

entries[0][0] === x;
entries[0][1] === x;
entries[1][0] === y;
entries[1][1] === y;
```

The keys() and values() iterators both yield a list of the unique values in the set. The entries() iterator yields a list of entry arrays, where both items of the array are the unique set value. The default iterator for a set is its values() iterator.

The inherent uniqueness of a set is its most useful trait. For example:

```
var s = new Set( [1,2,3,4,"1",2,4,"5"] ),
    uniques = [ ...s ];

uniques;                          // [1,2,3,4,"1","5"]
```

Set uniqueness does not allow coercion, so 1 and "1" are considered distinct values.

WeakSets

Whereas a WeakMap holds its keys weakly (but its values strongly), a WeakSet holds its values weakly (there aren't really keys).

```
var s = new WeakSet();

var x = { id: 1 },
    y = { id: 2 };

s.add( x );
s.add( y );

x = null;                    // `x` is GC-eligible
y = null;                    // `y` is GC-eligible
```

 WeakSet values must be objects, not primitive values as is allowed with sets.

Review

ES6 defines a number of useful collections that make working with data in structured ways more efficient and effective.

TypedArrays provide "view"s of binary data buffers that align with various integer types, like 8-bit unsigned integers and 32-bit floats. The array access to binary data makes operations much easier to express and maintain, which enables you to more easily work with complex data like video, audio, canvas data, and so on.

Maps are key-value pairs where the key can be an object instead of just a string/primitive. Sets are unique lists of values (of any type).

WeakMaps are maps where the key (object) is weakly held, so that GC is free to collect the entry if it's the last reference to an object. WeakSets are sets where the value is weakly held, again so that GC can remove the entry if it's the last reference to that object.

CHAPTER 6

API Additions

From conversions of values to mathematic calculations, ES6 adds many static properties and methods to various built-in natives and objects to help with common tasks. In addition, instances of some of the natives have new capabilities via various new prototype methods.

 Most of these features can be faithfully polyfilled. We will not dive into such details here, but check out "ES6 Shim" (*https://github.com/paul millr/es6-shim/*) for standards-compliant shims/polyfills.

Array

One of the most commonly extended features in JS by various user libraries is the Array type. It should be no surprise that ES6 adds a number of helpers to Array, both static and prototype (instance).

Array.of(..) Static Function

There's a well-known gotcha with the `Array(..)` constructor, which is that if there's only one argument passed, and that argument is a number, instead of making an array of one element with that number value in it, it constructs an empty array with a `length` property equal to the number. This action produces the unfortunate and quirky "empty slots" behavior that's reviled about JS arrays.

`Array.of(..)` replaces `Array(..)` as the preferred function-form constructor for arrays, because `Array.of(..)` does not have that special single-number-argument case. Consider:

```
var a = Array( 3 );
a.length;                   // 3
a[0];                       // undefined

var b = Array.of( 3 );
b.length;                   // 1
b[0];                       // 3

var c = Array.of( 1, 2, 3 );
c.length;                   // 3
c;                          // [1,2,3]
```

Under what circumstances would you want to use `Array.of(..)` instead of just creating an array with literal syntax, like `c = [1,2,3]`? There's two possible cases.

If you have a callback that's supposed to wrap argument(s) passed to it in an array, `Array.of(..)` fits the bill perfectly. That's probably not terribly common, but it may scratch an itch for you.

The other scenario is if you subclass `Array` (see "Classes" on page 135 in Chapter 3) and want to be able to create and initialize elements in an instance of your subclass, such as:

```
class MyCoolArray extends Array {
    sum() {
        return this.reduce( function reducer(acc,curr){
            return acc + curr;
        }, 0 );
    }
}

var x = new MyCoolArray( 3 );
x.length;                   // 3--oops!
x.sum();                    // 0--oops!

var y = [3];                // Array, not MyCoolArray
y.length;                   // 1
y.sum();                    // `sum` is not a function

var z = MyCoolArray.of( 3 );
z.length;                   // 1
z.sum();                    // 3
```

You can't just (easily) create a constructor for `MyCoolArray` that overrides the behavior of the `Array` parent constructor, because that constructor is necessary to actually create a well-behaving array value (initializing the this). The "inherited" static of(..) method on the MyCoolArray subclass provides a nice solution.

Array.from(..) Static Function

An "array-like object" in JavaScript is an object that has a length property on it, specifically with an integer value of zero or higher.

These values have been notoriously frustrating to work with in JS; it's been quite common to need to transform them into an actual array, so that the various Array.prototype methods (map(..), indexOf(..), etc.) are available to use with it. That process usually looks like:

```
// array-like object
var arrLike = {
    length: 3,
    0: "foo",
    1: "bar"
};

var arr = Array.prototype.slice.call( arrLike );
```

Another common task where slice(..) is often used is in duplicating a real array:

```
var arr2 = arr.slice();
```

In both cases, the new ES6 Array.from(..) method can be a more understandable and graceful—if also less verbose—approach:

```
var arr = Array.from( arrLike );

var arrCopy = Array.from( arr );
```

Array.from(..) looks to see if the first argument is an iterable (see "Iterators" on page 87 in Chapter 3), and if so, it uses the iterator to produce values to "copy" into the returned array. Because real arrays have an iterator for those values, that iterator is automatically used.

But if you pass an array-like object as the first argument to Array.from(..), it behaves basically the same as slice() (no arguments!) or apply(..) does, which is that it simply loops over the value, accessing numerically named properties from 0 up to whatever the value of length is.

Consider:

```
var arrLike = {
    length: 4,
    2: "foo"
};

Array.from( arrLike );
// [ undefined, undefined, "foo", undefined ]
```

Because positions 0, 1, and 3 didn't exist on arrLike, the result was the undefined value for each of those slots.

You could produce a similar outcome like this:

```
var emptySlotsArr = [];
emptySlotsArr.length = 4;
emptySlotsArr[2] = "foo";

Array.from( emptySlotsArr );
// [ undefined, undefined, "foo", undefined ]
```

Avoiding Empty Slots

There's a subtle but important difference in the previous snippet between the emptySlotsArr and the result of the Array.from(..) call. Array.from(..) never produces empty slots.

Prior to ES6, if you wanted to produce an array initialized to a certain length with actual undefined values in each slot (no empty slots!), you had to do extra work:

```
var a = Array( 4 );
// four empty slots!

var b = Array.apply( null, { length: 4 } );
// four `undefined` values
```

But Array.from(..) now makes this easier:

```
var c = Array.from( { length: 4 } );
// four `undefined` values
```

 Using an empty slot array like a in the previous snippets would work with some array functions, but others ignore empty slots (like map(..), etc.). You should never intentionally work with empty slots, as it will almost certainly lead to strange/unpredictable behavior in your programs.

Mapping

The `Array.from(..)` utility has another helpful trick up its sleeve. The second argument, if provided, is a mapping callback (almost the same as the regular `Array#map(..)` expects), which is called to map/transform each value from the source to the returned target. Consider:

```
var arrLike = {
    length: 4,
    2: "foo"
};

Array.from( arrLike, function mapper(val,idx){
    if (typeof val == "string") {
        return val.toUpperCase();
    }
    else {
        return idx;
    }
} );
// [ 0, 1, "FOO", 3 ]
```

 As with other array methods that take callbacks, `Array.from(..)` takes an optional third argument that if set will specify the `this` binding for the callback passed as the second argument. Otherwise, `this` will be `undefined`.

See "TypedArrays" on page 159 in Chapter 5 for an example of using `Array.from(..)` in translating values from an array of 8-bit values to an array of 16-bit values.

Creating Arrays and Subtypes

In the last couple of sections, we've discussed `Array.of(..)` and `Array.from(..)`, both of which create a new array in a similar way to a constructor. But what do they do in subclasses? Do they create instances of the base `Array` or the derived subclass?

```
class MyCoolArray extends Array {
    ..
}

MyCoolArray.from( [1, 2] ) instanceof MyCoolArray; // true

Array.from(
```

```
    MyCoolArray.from( [1, 2] )
) instanceof MyCoolArray;                            // false
```

Both of(..) and from(..) use the constructor that they're accessed from to construct the array. So if you use the base Array.of(..) you'll get an Array instance, but if you use MyCoolArray.of(..), you'll get a MyCoolArray instance.

In "Classes" on page 135 in Chapter 3, we covered the @@species setting that all the built-in classes (like Array) have defined, which is used by any prototype methods if they create a new instance. slice(..) is a great example:

```
var x = new MyCoolArray( 1, 2, 3 );

x.slice( 1 ) instanceof MyCoolArray;                 // true
```

Generally, that default behavior will probably be desired, but as we discussed in Chapter 3, you *can* override if you want:

```
class MyCoolArray extends Array {
    // force `species` to be parent constructor
    static get [Symbol.species]() { return Array; }
}

var x = new MyCoolArray( 1, 2, 3 );

x.slice( 1 ) instanceof MyCoolArray;                 // false
x.slice( 1 ) instanceof Array;                       // true
```

It's important to note that the @@species setting is only used for the prototype methods, like slice(..). It's not used by of(..) and from(..); they both just use the this binding (whatever constructor is used to make the reference). Consider:

```
class MyCoolArray extends Array {
    // force `species` to be parent constructor
    static get [Symbol.species]() { return Array; }
}

var x = new MyCoolArray( 1, 2, 3 );

MyCoolArray.from( x ) instanceof MyCoolArray;        // true
MyCoolArray.of( [2, 3] ) instanceof MyCoolArray;     // true
```

copyWithin(..) Prototype Method

Array#copyWithin(..) is a new mutator method available to all arrays (including typed arrays; see Chapter 5). copyWithin(..)

copies a portion of an array to another location in the same array, overwriting whatever was there before.

The arguments are *target* (the index to copy to), *start* (the inclusive index to start the copying from), and optionally *end* (the exclusive index to stop copying). If any of the arguments are negative, they're taken to be relative from the end of the array.

Consider:

```
[1,2,3,4,5].copyWithin( 3, 0 );         // [1,2,3,1,2]

[1,2,3,4,5].copyWithin( 3, 0, 1 );      // [1,2,3,1,5]

[1,2,3,4,5].copyWithin( 0, -2 );        // [4,5,3,4,5]

[1,2,3,4,5].copyWithin( 0, -2, -1 );    // [4,2,3,4,5]
```

The copyWithin(..) method does not extend the array's length, as the first example in the previous snippet shows. Copying simply stops when the end of the array is reached.

Contrary to what you might think, the copying doesn't always go in left-to-right (ascending index) order. It's possible this would result in repeatedly copying an already copied value if the from and target ranges overlap, which is presumably not desired behavior.

So internally, the algorithm avoids this case by copying in reverse order to avoid that gotcha. Consider:

```
[1,2,3,4,5].copyWithin( 2, 1 );     // ???
```

If the algorithm was strictly moving left to right, then the 2 should be copied to overwrite the 3, then *that* copied 2 should be copied to overwrite 4, then *that* copied 2 should be copied to overwrite 5, and you'd end up with [1,2,2,2,2].

Instead, the copying algorithm reverses direction and copies 4 to overwrite 5, then copies 3 to overwrite 4, then copies 2 to overwrite 3, and the final result is [1,2,2,3,4]. That's probably more "correct" in terms of expectation, but it can be confusing if you're only thinking about the copying algorithm in a naive left-to-right fashion.

fill(..) Prototype Method

Filling an existing array entirely (or partially) with a specified value is natively supported as of ES6 with the `Array#fill(..)` method:

```
var a = Array( 4 ).fill( undefined );
a;
// [undefined,undefined,undefined,undefined]
```

`fill(..)` optionally takes *start* and *end* parameters, which indicate a subset portion of the array to fill, such as:

```
var a = [ null, null, null, null ].fill( 42, 1, 3 );

a;                                      // [null,42,42,null]
```

find(..) Prototype Method

The most common way to search for a value in an array has generally been the `indexOf(..)` method, which returns the index the value is found at or -1 if not found:

```
var a = [1,2,3,4,5];

(a.indexOf( 3 ) != -1);                 // true
(a.indexOf( 7 ) != -1);                 // false

(a.indexOf( "2" ) != -1);               // false
```

The `indexOf(..)` comparison requires a strict `===` match, so a search for `"2"` fails to find a value of `2`, and vice versa. There's no way to override the matching algorithm for `indexOf(..)`. It's also unfortunate/ungraceful to have to make the manual comparison to the -1 value.

> See the *Types & Grammar* title of this series for an interesting (and controversially confusing) technique to work around the -1 ugliness with the ~ operator.

Since ES5, the most common workaround to have control over the matching logic has been the `some(..)` method. It works by calling a function callback for each element, until one of those calls returns a true/truthy value, and then it stops. Because you get to define the callback function, you have full control over how a match is made:

```
var a = [1,2,3,4,5];

a.some( function matcher(v){
    return v == "2";
} );                              // true

a.some( function matcher(v){
    return v == 7;
} );                              // false
```

But the downside to this approach is that you only get the true/false indicating if a suitably matched value was found, but not what the actual matched value was.

ES6's find(..) addresses this. It works basically the same as some(..), except that once the callback returns a true/truthy value, the actual array value is returned:

```
var a = [1,2,3,4,5];

a.find( function matcher(v){
    return v == "2";
} );                              // 2

a.find( function matcher(v){
    return v == 7;                // undefined
});
```

Using a custom matcher(..) function also lets you match against complex values like objects:

```
var points = [
    { x: 10, y: 20 },
    { x: 20, y: 30 },
    { x: 30, y: 40 },
    { x: 40, y: 50 },
    { x: 50, y: 60 }
];

points.find( function matcher(point) {
    return (
        point.x % 3 == 0 &&
        point.y % 4 == 0
    );
} );                              // { x: 30, y: 40 }
```

As with other array methods that take callbacks, find(..) takes an optional second argument that if set will specify the this binding for the callback passed as the first argument. Otherwise, this will be undefined.

findIndex(..) Prototype Method

While the previous section illustrates how some(..) yields a boolean result for a search of an array, and find(..) yields the matched value itself from the array search, there's also a need to find the positional index of the matched value.

indexOf(..) does that, but there's no control over its matching logic; it always uses === strict equality. So ES6's findIndex(..) is the answer:

```
var points = [
    { x: 10, y: 20 },
    { x: 20, y: 30 },
    { x: 30, y: 40 },
    { x: 40, y: 50 },
    { x: 50, y: 60 }
];

points.findIndex( function matcher(point) {
    return (
        point.x % 3 == 0 &&
        point.y % 4 == 0
    );
} );                                    // 2

points.findIndex( function matcher(point) {
    return (
        point.x % 6 == 0 &&
        point.y % 7 == 0
    );
} );                                    // -1
```

Don't use findIndex(..) != -1 (the way it's always been done with indexOf(..)) to get a boolean from the search, because some(..) already yields the true/false you want. And don't do a[a.findIndex(..)] to get the matched value, because that's what find(..) accomplishes. And finally, use indexOf(..) if you need the index of a strict match, or findIndex(..) if you need the index of a more customized match.

As with other array methods that take callbacks, find(..) takes an optional second argument that if set will specify the this binding for the callback passed as the first argument. Otherwise, this will be undefined.

entries(), values(), keys() Prototype Methods

In Chapter 3, we illustrated how data structures can provide a patterned item-by-item enumeration of their values, via an iterator. We then expounded on this approach in Chapter 5, as we explored how the new ES6 collections (Map, Set, etc.) provide several methods for producing different kinds of iterations.

Because it's not new to ES6, Array might not be thought of traditionally as a "collection," but it is one in the sense that it provides these same iterator methods: entries(), values(), and keys(). Consider:

```
var a = [1,2,3];

[...a.values()];              // [1,2,3]
[...a.keys()];                // [0,1,2]
[...a.entries()];             // [ [0,1], [1,2], [2,3] ]

[...a[Symbol.iterator]()];    // [1,2,3]
```

Just like with Set, the default Array iterator is the same as what values() returns.

In "String Inspection Functions" on page 196, we illustrated how Array.from(..) treats empty slots in an array as just being present slots with undefined in them. That's actually because under the covers, the array iterators behave that way:

```
var a = [];
a.length = 3;
a[1] = 2;

[...a.values()];    // [undefined,2,undefined]
[...a.keys()];      // [0,1,2]
[...a.entries()];   // [ [0,undefined], [1,2], [2,undefined] ]
```

Object

A few additional static helpers have been added to `Object`. Traditionally, functions of this sort have been seen as focused on the behaviors/capabilities of object values.

However, starting with ES6, `Object` static functions will also be for general-purpose global APIs of any sort that don't already belong more naturally in some other location (i.e., `Array.from(..)`).

Object.is(..) Static Function

The `Object.is(..)` static function makes value comparisons in an even more strict fashion than the `===` comparison.

`Object.is(..)` invokes the underlying `SameValue` algorithm (ES6 spec, section 7.2.9). The `SameValue` algorithm is basically the same as the `===` Strict Equality Comparison Algorithm (ES6 spec, section 7.2.13), with two important exceptions.

Consider:

```
var x = NaN, y = 0, z = -0;

x === x;                    // false
y === z;                    // true

Object.is( x, x );          // true
Object.is( y, z );          // false
```

You should continue to use `===` for strict equality comparisons; `Object.is(..)` shouldn't be thought of as a replacement for the operator. However, in cases where you're trying to strictly identify a `NaN` or `-0` value, `Object.is(..)` is now the preferred option.

 ES6 also adds a `Number.isNaN(..)` utility (discussed later in this chapter), which may be a slightly more convenient test; you may prefer `Number.isNaN(x)` over `Object.is(x,NaN)`. You *can* accurately test for `-0` with a clumsy `x == 0 && 1 / x === -Infinity`, but in this case `Object.is(x,-0)` is much better.

Object.getOwnPropertySymbols(..) Static Function

"Symbols" on page 80 in Chapter 2 discusses the new Symbol primitive value type in ES6.

Symbols are likely going to be mostly used as special (meta) properties on objects. So the `Object.getOwnPropertySymbols(..)` utility was introduced, which retrieves only the symbol properties directly on an object:

```
var o = {
    foo: 42,
    [ Symbol( "bar" ) ]: "hello world",
    baz: true
};

Object.getOwnPropertySymbols( o );  // [ Symbol(bar) ]
```

Object.setPrototypeOf(..) Static Function

Also in Chapter 2, we mentioned the `Object.setPrototypeOf(..)` utility, which (unsurprisingly) sets the `[[Prototype]]` of an object for the purposes of *behavior delegation* (see the *this & Object Prototypes* title of this series). Consider:

```
var o1 = {
    foo() { console.log( "foo" ); }
};
var o2 = {
    // .. o2's definition ..
};

Object.setPrototypeOf( o2, o1 );

// delegates to `o1.foo()`
o2.foo();                           // foo
```

Alternatively:

```
var o1 = {
    foo() { console.log( "foo" ); }
};

var o2 = Object.setPrototypeOf( {
    // .. o2's definition ..
}, o1 );

// delegates to `o1.foo()`
o2.foo();                           // foo
```

In both previous snippets, the relationship between o2 and o1 appears at the end of the o2 definition. More commonly, the relationship between an o2 and o1 is specified at the top of the o2 definition, as it is with classes, and also with __proto__ in object literals (see "Setting [[Prototype]]" on page 45 in Chapter 2).

> Setting a [[Prototype]] right after object creation is reasonable, as shown. But changing it much later is generally not a good idea and will usually lead to more confusion than clarity.

Object.assign(..) Static Function

Many JavaScript libraries/frameworks provide utilities for copying/mixing one object's properties into another (e.g., jQuery's extend(..)). There are various nuanced differences between these different utilities, such as whether a property with value undefined is ignored or not.

ES6 adds Object.assign(..), which is a simplified version of these algorithms. The first argument is the *target*, and any other arguments passed are the *sources*, which will be processed in listed order. For each source, its enumerable and own (e.g., not "inherited") keys, including symbols, are copied as if by plain = assignment. Object.assign(..) returns the target object.

Consider this object setup:

```
var target = {},
    o1 = { a: 1 }, o2 = { b: 2 },
    o3 = { c: 3 }, o4 = { d: 4 };

// set up read-only property
Object.defineProperty( o3, "e", {
    value: 5,
    enumerable: true,
    writable: false,
    configurable: false
} );

// set up non-enumerable property
Object.defineProperty( o3, "f", {
    value: 6,
    enumerable: false
} );
```

```
o3[ Symbol( "g" ) ] = 7;

// set up non-enumerable symbol
Object.defineProperty( o3, Symbol( "h" ), {
    value: 8,
    enumerable: false
} );

Object.setPrototypeOf( o3, o4 );
```

Only the properties a, b, c, e, and Symbol("g") will be copied to tar
get:

```
Object.assign( target, o1, o2, o3 );

target.a;                               // 1
target.b;                               // 2
target.c;                               // 3

Object.getOwnPropertyDescriptor( target, "e" );
// { value: 5, writable: true, enumerable: true,
//   configurable: true }

Object.getOwnPropertySymbols( target );
// [Symbol("g")]
```

The d, f, and Symbol("h") properties are omitted from copying;
non-enumerable properties and non-owned properties are all exclu-
ded from the assignment. Also, e is copied as a normal property
assignment, not duplicated as a read-only property.

In an earlier section, we showed using setPrototypeOf(..) to set
up a [[Prototype]] relationship between an o2 and o1 object.
There's another form that leverages Object.assign(..):

```
var o1 = {
    foo() { console.log( "foo" ); }
};

var o2 = Object.assign(
    Object.create( o1 ),
    {
        // .. o2's definition ..
    }
);

// delegates to `o1.foo()`
o2.foo();                               // foo
```

`Object.create(..)` is the ES5 standard utility that creates an empty object that is [[Prototype]]-linked. See the *this & Object Prototypes* title of this series for more information.

Math

ES6 adds several new mathematic utilities that fill in holes or aid with common operations. All of these can be manually calculated, but most of them are now defined natively so that in some cases the JS engine can either more optimally perform the calculations, or perform them with better decimal precision than their manual counterparts.

It's likely that asm.js/transpiled JS code (see the *Async & Performance* title of this series) is the more likely consumer of many of these utilities rather than direct developers.

Trigonometry:

`cosh(..)`
> Hyperbolic cosine

`acosh(..)`
> Hyperbolic arccosine

`sinh(..)`
> Hyperbolic sine

`asinh(..)`
> Hyperbolic arcsine

`tanh(..)`
> Hyperbolic tangent

`atanh(..)`
> Hyperbolic arctangent

`hypot(..)`
> The squareroot of the sum of the squares (i.e., the generalized Pythagorean theorem)

Arithmetic:

`cbrt(..)`
Cube root

`clz32(..)`
Count leading zeros in 32-bit binary representation

`expm1(..)`
The same as `exp(x) - 1`

`log2(..)`
Binary logarithm (log base 2)

`log10(..)`
Log base 10

`log1p(..)`
The same as `log(x + 1)`

`imul(..)`
32-bit integer multiplication of two numbers

Meta:

`sign(..)`
Returns the sign of the number

`trunc(..)`
Returns only the integer part of a number

`fround(..)`
Rounds to nearest 32-bit (single precision) floating-point value

Number

Importantly, for your program to properly work, it must accurately handle numbers. ES6 adds some additional properties and functions to assist with common numeric operations.

Two additions to `Number` are just references to the pre-existing globals: `Number.parseInt(..)` and `Number.parseFloat(..)`.

Static Properties

ES6 adds some helpful numeric constants as static properties:

`Number.EPSILON`

The minimum value between any two numbers: `2^-52` (see Chapter 2 of the *Types & Grammar* title of this series regarding using this value as a tolerance for imprecision in floating-point arithmetic)

`Number.MAX_SAFE_INTEGER`

The highest integer that can "safely" be represented unambiguously in a JS number value: `2^53 - 1`

`Number.MIN_SAFE_INTEGER`

The lowest integer that can "safely" be represented unambiguously in a JS number value: `-(2^53 - 1)` or `(-2)^53 + 1`

 See Chapter 2 of the *Types & Grammar* title of this series for more information about "safe" integers.

Number.isNaN(..) Static Function

The standard global `isNaN(..)` utility has been broken since its inception, in that it returns `true` for things that are not numbers, not just for the actual `NaN` value, because it coerces the argument to a number type (which can falsely result in a `NaN`). ES6 adds a fixed utility `Number.isNaN(..)` that works as it should:

```
var a = NaN, b = "NaN", c = 42;

isNaN( a );                      // true
isNaN( b );                      // true--oops!
isNaN( c );                      // false

Number.isNaN( a );               // true
Number.isNaN( b );               // false--fixed!
Number.isNaN( c );               // false
```

Number.isFinite(..) Static Function

There's a temptation to look at a function name like `isFinite(..)` and assume it's simply "not infinite". That's not quite correct, though. There's more nuance to this new ES6 utility. Consider:

```
var a = NaN, b = Infinity, c = 42;
```

```
Number.isFinite( a );          // false
Number.isFinite( b );          // false

Number.isFinite( c );          // true
```

The standard global isFinite(..) coerces its argument, but Num
ber.isFinite(..) omits the coercive behavior:

```
var a = "42";

isFinite( a );                 // true
Number.isFinite( a );          // false
```

You may still prefer the coercion, in which case using the global
isFinite(..) is a valid choice. Alternatively, and perhaps more sen-
sibly, you can use Number.isFinite(+x), which explicitly coerces x
to a number before passing it in (see Chapter 4 of the *Types &*
Grammar title of this series).

Integer-Related Static Functions

JavaScript number valuess are always floating point (IEE-754). So
the notion of determining if a number is an "integer" is not about
checking its type, because JS makes no such distinction.

Instead, you need to check if there's any nonzero decimal portion of
the value. The easiest way to do that has commonly been:

```
x === Math.floor( x );
```

ES6 adds a Number.isInteger(..) helper utility that potentially can
determine this quality slightly more efficiently:

```
Number.isInteger( 4 );         // true
Number.isInteger( 4.2 );       // false
```

 In JavaScript, there's no difference between 4, 4.,
4.0, or 4.0000. All of these would be considered
an "integer," and would thus yield true from
Number.isInteger(..).

In addition, Number.isInteger(..) filters out some clearly not-
integer values that x === Math.floor(x) could potentially mix up:

```
Number.isInteger( NaN );       // false
Number.isInteger( Infinity );  // false
```

Working with "integers" is sometimes an important bit of information, as it can simplify certain kinds of algorithms. JS code by itself will not run faster just from filtering for only integers, but there are optimization techniques the engine can take (e.g., asm.js) when only integers are being used.

Because of `Number.isInteger(..)`'s handling of `NaN` and `Infinity` values, defining a `isFloat(..)` utility would not be just as simple as `!Number.isInteger(..)`. You'd need to do something like:

```
function isFloat(x) {
    return Number.isFinite( x ) && !Number.isInteger( x );
}

isFloat( 4.2 );                 // true
isFloat( 4 );                   // false

isFloat( NaN );                 // false
isFloat( Infinity );            // false
```

It may seem strange, but `Infinity` should neither be considered an integer nor a float.

ES6 also defines a `Number.isSafeInteger(..)` utility, which checks to make sure the value is both an integer and within the range of `Number.MIN_SAFE_INTEGER`-`Number.MAX_SAFE_INTEGER` (inclusive).

```
var x = Math.pow( 2, 53 ),
    y = Math.pow( -2, 53 );

Number.isSafeInteger( x - 1 );          // true
Number.isSafeInteger( y + 1 );          // true

Number.isSafeInteger( x );              // false
Number.isSafeInteger( y );              // false
```

String

Strings already have quite a few helpers prior to ES6, but even more have been added to the mix.

Unicode Functions

"Unicode-Aware String Operations" on page 75 in Chapter 2 discusses `String.fromCodePoint(..)`, `String#codePointAt(..)`, and `String#normalize(..)` in detail. They have been added to improve Unicode support in JS string values.

```
String.fromCodePoint( 0x1d49e );          // "𝒞"
"ab𝒞d.codePointAt( 2 ).toString( 16 );   // "1d49e"
```

The `normalize(..)` string prototype method is used to perform Unicode normalizations that either combine characters with adjacent "combining marks" or decompose combined characters.

Generally, the normalization won't create a visible effect on the contents of the string, but will change the contents of the string, which can affect how things like the `length` property are reported, as well as how character access by position behaves:

```
var s1 = "e\u0301";
s1.length;                    // 2

var s2 = s1.normalize();
s2.length;                    // 1
s2 === "\xE9";                // true
```

`normalize(..)` takes an optional argument that specifies the normalization form to use. This argument must be one of the following four values: `"NFC"` (default), `"NFD"`, `"NFKC"`, or `"NFKD"`.

> Normalization forms and their effects on strings is well beyond the scope of what we'll discuss here. See "Unicode Normalization Forms" (*http://www.unicode.org/reports/tr15/*) for more information.

String.raw(..) Static Function

The `String.raw(..)` utility is provided as a built-in tag function to use with template string literals (see Chapter 2) for obtaining the raw string value without any processing of escape sequences.

This function will almost never be called manually, but will be used with tagged template literals:

```
var str = "bc";

String.raw`\ta${str}d\xE9`;
// "\tabcd\xE9", not "	abcdé"
```

In the resultant string, \ and t are separate raw characters, not the one escape sequence character \t. The same is true of the Unicode escape sequence.

repeat(..) Prototype Function

In languages like Python and Ruby, you can repeat a string as:

```
"foo" * 3;                       // "foofoofoo"
```

That doesn't work in JS, because * multiplication is only defined for numbers, and thus "foo" coerces to the NaN number.

However, ES6 defines a string prototype method repeat(..) to accomplish the task:

```
"foo".repeat( 3 );               // "foofoofoo"
```

String Inspection Functions

In addition to String#indexOf(..) and String#lastIndexOf(..) from prior to ES6, three new methods for searching/inspection have been added: startsWith(..), endsWidth(..), and includes(..).

```
var palindrome = "step on no pets";

palindrome.startsWith( "step on" ); // true
palindrome.startsWith( "on", 5 );   // true

palindrome.endsWith( "no pets" );   // true
palindrome.endsWith( "no", 10 );    // true

palindrome.includes( "on" );        // true
palindrome.includes( "on", 6 );     // false
```

For all the string search/inspection methods, if you look for an empty string "", it will either be found at the beginning or the end of the string.

 These methods will not by default accept a regular expression for the search string. See "Regular Expression Symbols" on page 208 in Chapter 7 for information about disabling the isRegExp check that is performed on this first argument.

Review

ES6 adds many extra API helpers on the various built-in native objects:

- `Array` adds `of(..)` and `from(..)` static functions, as well as prototype functions like `copyWithin(..)` and `fill(..)`.
- `Object` adds static functions like `is(..)` and `assign(..)`.
- `Math` adds static functions like `acosh(..)` and `clz32(..)`.
- `Number` adds static properties like `Number.EPSILON`, as well as static functions like `Number.isFinite(..)`.
- `String` adds static functions like `String.fromCodePoint(..)` and `String.raw(..)`, as well as prototype functions like `repeat(..)` and `includes(..)`.

Most of these additions can be polyfilled (see ES6 Shim), and were inspired by utilities in common JS libraries/frameworks.

CHAPTER 7

Meta Programming

Meta programming is programming where the operation targets the behavior of the program itself. In other words, it's programming the programming of your program. Yeah, a mouthful, huh?

For example, if you probe the relationship between one object a and another b—are they [[Prototype]] linked?—using a.isProto type(b), this is commonly referred to as introspection, a form of meta programming. Macros (which don't exist in JS, yet)—where the code modifies itself at compile time—are another obvious example of meta programming. Enumerating the keys of an object with a for..in loop, or checking if an object is an *instance of* a "class constructor," are other common meta programming tasks.

Meta programming focuses on one or more of the following: code inspecting itself, code modifying itself, or code modifying default language behavior so other code is affected.

The goal of meta programming is to leverage the language's own intrinsic capabilities to make the rest of your code more descriptive, expressive, and/or flexible. Because of the *meta* nature of meta programming, it's somewhat difficult to put a more precise definition on it than that. The best way to understand meta programming is to see it through examples.

ES6 adds several new forms/features for meta programming on top of what JS already had.

Function Names

There are cases where your code may want to introspect on itself and ask what the name of some function is. If you ask what a function's name is, the answer is surprisingly somewhat ambiguous. Consider:

```
function daz() {
    // ..
}

var obj = {
    foo: function() {
        // ..
    },
    bar: function baz() {
        // ..
    },
    bam: daz,
    zim() {
        // ..
    }
};
```

In this previous snippet, "what is the name of obj.foo()" is slightly nuanced. Is it "foo", "", or undefined? And what about obj.bar() —is it named "bar" or "baz"? Is obj.bam() named "bam" or "daz"? What about obj.zim()?

Moreover, what about functions that are passed as callbacks, like:

```
function foo(cb) {
    // what is the name of `cb()` here?
}

foo( function(){
    // I'm anonymous!
} );
```

There are quite a few ways that functions can be expressed in programs, and it's not always clear and unambiguous what the "name" of that function should be.

More importantly, we need to distinguish whether the "name" of a function refers to its name property—yes, functions have a property called name—or whether it refers to the lexical binding name, such as bar in function bar() { .. }.

The lexical binding name is what you use for things like recursion:

```
function foo(i) {
    if (i < 10) return foo( i * 2 );
    return i;
}
```

The `name` property is what you'd use for meta programming purposes, so that's what we'll focus on in this discussion.

The confusion comes because by default, the lexical name a function has (if any) is also set as its `name` property. Actually, there was no official requirement for that behavior by the ES5 (and prior) specifications. The setting of the `name` property was nonstandard but still fairly reliable. As of ES6, it has been standardized.

 If a function has a `name` value assigned, that's typically the name used in stack traces in developer tools.

Inferences

But what happens to the `name` property if a function has no lexical name?

As of ES6, there are now inference rules that can determine a sensible `name` property value to assign a function even if that function doesn't have a lexical name to use.

Consider:

```
var abc = function() {
    // ..
};

abc.name;                // "abc"
```

Had we given the function a lexical name like `abc = function def() { .. }`, the `name` property would of course be `"def"`. But in the absence of the lexical name, intuitively the `"abc"` name seems appropriate.

Here are other forms that will infer a name (or not) in ES6:

```
(function(){ .. });              // name:
(function*(){ .. });             // name:
window.foo = function(){ .. };   // name:

class Awesome {
```

```
    constructor() { .. }          // name: Awesome
    funny() { .. }                // name: funny
}

var c = class Awesome { .. };     // name: Awesome

var o = {
    foo() { .. },                 // name: foo
    *bar() { .. },                // name: bar
    baz: () => { .. },            // name: baz
    bam: function(){ .. },        // name: bam
    get qux() { .. },             // name: get qux
    set fuz() { .. },             // name: set fuz
    ["b" + "iz"]:
        function(){ .. },         // name: biz
    [Symbol( "buz" )]:
        function(){ .. }          // name: [buz]
};

var x = o.foo.bind( o );          // name: bound foo
(function(){ .. }).bind( o );     // name: bound

export default function() { .. }  // name: default

var y = new Function();           // name: anonymous
var GeneratorFunction =
    function*(){}.__proto__.constructor;
var z = new GeneratorFunction();  // name: anonymous
```

The `name` property is not writable by default, but it is configurable,
meaning you can use `Object.defineProperty(..)` to manually
change it if so desired.

Meta Properties

In "new.target" on page 143 in Chapter 3, we introduced a concept
new to JS in ES6: the meta property. As the name suggests, meta
properties are intended to provide special meta information in the
form of a property access that would otherwise not have been possible.

In the case of `new.target`, the keyword `new` serves as the context for
a property access. Clearly `new` is itself not an object, which makes
this capability special. However, when `new.target` is used inside a
constructor call (a function/method invoked with `new`), `new` becomes
a virtual context, so that `new.target` can refer to the target constructor that `new` invoked.

This is a clear example of a meta programming operation, as the intent is to determine from inside a constructor call what the original new target was, generally for the purposes of introspection (examining typing/structure) or static property access.

For example, you may want to have different behavior in a constructor depending on if it's directly invoked or invoked via a child class:

```
class Parent {
    constructor() {
        if (new.target === Parent) {
            console.log( "Parent instantiated" );
        }
        else {
            console.log( "A child instantiated" );
        }
    }
}

class Child extends Parent {}

var a = new Parent();
// Parent instantiated

var b = new Child();
// A child instantiated
```

There's a slight nuance here, which is that the `constructor()` inside the `Parent` class definition is actually given the lexical name of the class (`Parent`), even though the syntax implies that the class is a separate entity from the constructor.

 As with all meta programming techniques, be careful of creating code that's too clever for your future self or others maintaining your code to understand. Use these tricks with caution.

Well-Known Symbols

In "Symbols" on page 80 in Chapter 2, we covered the new ES6 primitive type `symbol`. In addition to symbols you can define in your own program, JS predefines a number of built-in symbols, referred to as *Well-Known Symbols* (WKS).

These symbol values are defined primarily to expose special meta properties that are being exposed to your JS programs to give you more control over JS's behavior.

We'll briefly introduce each and discuss their purpose.

Symbol.iterator

In Chapters 2 and 3, we introduced and used the `@@iterator` symbol, automatically used by `...` spreads and `for..of` loops. We also saw `@@iterator` as defined on the new ES6 collections as defined in Chapter 5.

`Symbol.iterator` represents the special location (property) on any object where the language mechanisms automatically look to find a method that will construct an iterator instance for consuming that object's values. Many objects come with a default one defined.

However, we can define our own iterator logic for any object value by setting the `Symbol.iterator` property, even if that's overriding the default iterator. The meta programming aspect is that we are defining behavior that other parts of JS (namely, operators and looping constructs) use when processing an object value we define.

Consider:

```
var arr = [4,5,6,7,8,9];

for (var v of arr) {
    console.log( v );
}
// 4 5 6 7 8 9

// define iterator that only produces values
// from odd indexes
arr[Symbol.iterator] = function*() {
    var idx = 1;
    do {
        yield this[idx];
    } while ((idx += 2) < this.length);
};

for (var v of arr) {
    console.log( v );
}
// 5 7 9
```

Symbol.toStringTag and Symbol.hasInstance

One of the most common meta programming tasks is to introspect on a value to find out what *kind* it is, usually to decide what operations are appropriate to perform on it. With objects, the two most common inspection techniques are toString() and instanceof.

Consider:

```
function Foo() {}

var a = new Foo();

a.toString();              // [object Object]
a instanceof Foo;          // true
```

As of ES6, you can control the behavior of these operations:

```
function Foo(greeting) {
    this.greeting = greeting;
}

Foo.prototype[Symbol.toStringTag] = "Foo";

Object.defineProperty( Foo, Symbol.hasInstance, {
    value: function(inst) {
        return inst.greeting == "hello";
    }
} );

var a = new Foo( "hello" ),
    b = new Foo( "world" );

b[Symbol.toStringTag] = "cool";

a.toString();              // [object Foo]
String( b );               // [object cool]

a instanceof Foo;          // true
b instanceof Foo;          // false
```

The @@toStringTag symbol on the prototype (or instance itself) specifies a string value to use in the [object ____] stringification.

The @@hasInstance symbol is a method on the constructor function which receives the instance object value and lets you decide by returning true or false if the value should be considered an instance or not.

To set @@hasInstance on a function, you must use Object.defineProperty(..), as the default one on Function.prototype is writable: false. See the *this & Object Prototypes* title of this series for more information.

Symbol.species

In "Classes" on page 135 in Chapter 3, we introduced the @@species symbol, which controls which constructor is used by built-in methods of a class that needs to spawn new instances.

The most common example is when subclassing Array and wanting to define which constructor (Array(..) or your subclass) inherited methods like slice(..) should use. By default, slice(..) called on an instance of a subclass of Array would produce a new instance of that subclass, which is frankly what you'll likely often want.

However, you can meta program by overriding a class's default @@species definition:

```
class Cool {
    // defer `@@species` to derived constructor
    static get [Symbol.species]() { return this; }

    again() {
        return new this.constructor[Symbol.species]();
    }
}

class Fun extends Cool {}

class Awesome extends Cool {
    // force `@@species` to be parent constructor
    static get [Symbol.species]() { return Cool; }
}

var a = new Fun(),
    b = new Awesome(),
    c = a.again(),
    d = b.again();

c instanceof Fun;           // true
d instanceof Awesome;       // false
d instanceof Cool;          // true
```

The Symbol.species setting defaults on the built-in native constructors to the return this behavior as illustrated in the previous snippet in the `Cool` definition. It has no default on user classes, but as shown that behavior is easy to emulate.

If you need to define methods that generate new instances, use the meta programming of the `new this.constructor[Symbol.spe cies](..)` pattern instead of the hard-wiring of `new this.construc tor(..)` or `new XYZ(..)`. Derived classes will then be able to customize `Symbol.species` to control which constructor vends those instances.

Symbol.toPrimitive

In the *Types & Grammar* title of this series, we discussed the `ToPri mitive` abstract coercion operation, which is used when an object must be coerced to a primitive value for some operation (such as == comparison or + addition). Prior to ES6, there was no way to control this behavior.

As of ES6, the `@@toPrimitive` symbol as a property on any object value can customize that `ToPrimitive` coercion by specifying a method.

Consider:

```
var arr = [1,2,3,4,5];

arr + 10;                // 1,2,3,4,510

arr[Symbol.toPrimitive] = function(hint) {
    if (hint == "default" || hint == "number") {
        // sum all numbers
        return this.reduce( function(acc,curr){
            return acc + curr;
        }, 0 );
    }
};

arr + 10;                // 25
```

The `Symbol.toPrimitive` method will be provided with a *hint* of `"string"`, `"number"`, or `"default"` (which should be interpreted as `"number"`), depending on what type the operation invoking `ToPrimi tive` is expecting. In the previous snippet, the additive + operation has no hint ("default" is passed). A multiplicative * operation would hint `"number"` and a `String(arr)` would hint `"string"`.

The == operator will invoke the ToPrimitive operation with no hint—the @@toPrimitive method, if any is called with hint "default"—on an object if the other value being compared is not an object. However, if both comparison values are objects, the behavior of == is identical to ===, which is that the references themselves are directly compared. In this case, @@toPrimitive is not invoked at all. See the *Types & Grammar* title of this series for more information about coercion and the abstract operations.

Regular Expression Symbols

There are four well-known symbols that can be overridden for regular expression objects, which control how those regular expressions are used by the four corresponding String.prototype functions of the same name:

- @@match: The Symbol.match value of a regular expression is the method used to match all or part of a string value with the given regular expression. It's used by String.prototype.match(..) if you pass it a regular expression for the pattern matching.

The default algorithm for matching is laid out in section 21.2.5.6 of the ES6 specification (*https://people.mozilla.org/~jorendorff/es6-draft.html#sec-regexp.prototype-@@match*). You could override this default algorithm and provide extra regex features, such as look-behind assertions.

Symbol.match is also used by the isRegExp abstract operation (see the note in "String Inspection Functions" on page 196 in Chapter 6) to determine if an object is intended to be used as a regular expression. To force this check to fail for an object so it's not treated as a regular expression, set the Symbol.match value to false (or something falsy). * @@replace: The Symbol.replace value of a regular expression is the method used by String.prototype.replace(..) to replace within a string one or all occurrences of character sequences that match the given regular expression pattern.

The default algorithm for replacing is laid out in section 21.2.5.8 of the ES6 specification (*https://people.mozilla.org/~jorendorff/es6-draft.html#sec-regexp.prototype-@@replace*).

One cool use for overriding the default algorithm is to provide additional `replacer` argument options, such as supporting `"abaca".replace(/a/g,[1,2,3])` producing `"1b2c3"` by consuming the iterable for successive replacement values. * `@@search`: The `Symbol.search` value of a regular expression is the method used by `String.prototype.search(..)` to search for a substring within another string as matched by the given regular expression.

The default algorithm for searching is laid out in section 21.2.5.9 of the ES6 specification (*https://people.mozilla.org/~jorendorff/es6-draft.html#sec-regexp.prototype-@@search*). * `@@split`: The `Symbol.split` value of a regular expression is the method used by `String.prototype.split(..)` to split a string into substrings at the location(s) of the delimiter as matched by the given regular expression.

The default algorithm for splitting is laid out in section 21.2.5.11 of the ES6 specification (*https://people.mozilla.org/~jorendorff/es6-draft.html#sec-regexp.prototype-@@split*).

Overriding the built-in regular expression algorithms is not for the faint of heart! JS ships with a highly optimized regular expression engine, so your own user code will likely be a lot slower. This kind of meta programming is neat and powerful, but it should only be used in cases where it's really necessary or beneficial.

Symbol.isConcatSpreadable

The `@@isConcatSpreadable` symbol can be defined as a boolean property (`Symbol.isConcatSpreadable`) on any object (like an array or other iterable) to indicate if it should be *spread out* if passed to an array `concat(..)`.

Consider:

```
var a = [1,2,3],
    b = [4,5,6];

b[Symbol.isConcatSpreadable] = false;

[].concat( a, b );      // [1,2,3,[4,5,6]]
```

Symbol.unscopables

The @@unscopables symbol can be defined as an object property (Symbol.unscopables) on any object to indicate which properties can and cannot be exposed as lexical variables in a with statement.

Consider:

```
var o = { a:1, b:2, c:3 },
    a = 10, b = 20, c = 30;

o[Symbol.unscopables] = {
    a: false,
    b: true,
    c: false
};

with (o) {
    console.log( a, b, c );    // 1 20 3
}
```

A true in the @@unscopables object indicates the property should be *unscopable*, and thus filtered out from the lexical scope variables. false means it's OK to be included in the lexical scope variables.

 The with statement is disallowed entirely in strict mode, and as such should be considered deprecated from the language. Don't use it. See the *Scope & Closures* title of this series for more information. Because with should be avoided, the @@unscopables symbol is also moot.

Proxies

One of the most obviously meta programming features added to ES6 is the Proxy feature.

A proxy is a special kind of object you create that "wraps"—or sits in front of—another normal object. You can register special handlers (aka *traps*) on the proxy object, which are called when various operations are performed against the proxy. These handlers have the opportunity to perform extra logic in addition to *forwarding* the operations on to the original target/wrapped object.

One example of the kind of *trap* handler you can define on a proxy is get that intercepts the [[Get]] operation—performed when you try to access a property on an object. Consider:

```
var obj = { a: 1 },
    handlers = {
        get(target,key,context) {
            // note: target === obj,
            // context === pobj
            console.log( "accessing: ", key );
            return Reflect.get(
                target, key, context
            );
        }
    },
    pobj = new Proxy( obj, handlers );

obj.a;
// 1

pobj.a;
// accessing: a
// 1
```

We declare a get(..) handler as a named method on the *handler* object (second argument to Proxy(..)), that receives a reference to the *target* object (obj), the *key* property name ("a"), and the self/receiver/proxy (pobj).

After the console.log(..) tracing statement, we "forward" the operation onto obj via Reflect.get(..). We will cover the Reflect API in the next section, but note that each available proxy trap has a corresponding Reflect function of the same name.

These mappings are symmetric on purpose. The proxy handlers each intercept when a respective meta programming task is performed, and the Reflect utilities each perform the respective meta programming task on an object. Each proxy handler has a default definition that automatically calls the corresponding Reflect utility. You will almost certainly use both Proxy and Reflect in tandem.

Here's a list of handlers you can define on a proxy for a *target* object/function, and how/when they are triggered:

get(..)
> Via [[Get]], a property is accessed on the proxy (Reflect.get(..), . property operator, or [..] property operator)

set(..)
> Via [[Set]], a property value is set on the proxy (Reflect.set(..), the = assignment operator, or destructuring assignment if it targets an object property)

deleteProperty(..)
> Via [[Delete]], a property is deleted from the proxy (Reflect.deleteProperty(..) or delete)

apply(..) *(if target is a function)*
> Via [[Call]], the proxy is invoked as a normal function/method (Reflect.apply(..), call(..), apply(..), or the (..) call operator)

construct(..) *(if target is a constructor function)*
> Via [[Construct]], the proxy is invoked as a constructor function (Reflect.construct(..) or new)

getOwnPropertyDescriptor(..)
> Via [[GetOwnProperty]], a property descriptor is retrieved from the proxy (Object.getOwnPropertyDescriptor(..) or Reflect.getOwnPropertyDescriptor(..))

defineProperty(..)
> Via [[DefineOwnProperty]], a property descriptor is set on the proxy (Object.defineProperty(..) or Reflect.defineProperty(..))

getPrototypeOf(..)
> Via [[GetPrototypeOf]], the [[Prototype]] of the proxy is retrieved (Object.getPrototypeOf(..), Reflect.getPrototypeOf(..), __proto__, Object#isPrototypeOf(..), or instanceof)

setPrototypeOf(..)
> Via [[SetPrototypeOf]], the [[Prototype]] of the proxy is set (Object.setPrototypeOf(..), Reflect.setPrototypeOf(..), or __proto__)

`preventExtensions(..)`

Via `[[PreventExtensions]]`, the proxy is made non-extensible (`Object.preventExtensions(..)` or `Reflect.preventExtensions(..)`)

`isExtensible(..)`

Via `[[IsExtensible]]`, the extensibility of the proxy is probed (`Object.isExtensible(..)` or `Reflect.isExtensible(..)`)

`ownKeys(..)`

Via `[[OwnPropertyKeys]]`, the set of owned properties and/or owned symbol properties of the proxy is retrieved (`Object.keys(..)`, `Object.getOwnPropertyNames(..)`, `Object.getOwnSymbolProperties(..)`, `Reflect.ownKeys(..)`, or `JSON.stringify(..)`)

`enumerate(..)`

Via `[[Enumerate]]`, an iterator is requested for the proxy's enumerable owned and "inherited" properties (`Reflect.enumerate(..)` or `for..in`)

`has(..)`

Via `[[HasProperty]]`, the proxy is probed to see if it has an owned or "inherited" property (`Reflect.has(..)`, `Object#hasOwnProperty(..)`, or `"prop" in obj`)

 For more information about each of these meta programming tasks, see "Reflect API" on page 224 later in this chapter.

In addition to the notations in the preceding list about actions that will trigger the various traps, some traps are triggered indirectly by the default actions of another trap. For example:

```
var handlers = {
    getOwnPropertyDescriptor(target,prop) {
        console.log(
            "getOwnPropertyDescriptor"
        );
        return Object.getOwnPropertyDescriptor(
            target, prop
        );
    },
```

```
        defineProperty(target,prop,desc){
            console.log( "defineProperty" );
            return Object.defineProperty(
                target, prop, desc
            );
        }
    },
    proxy = new Proxy( {}, handlers );

proxy.a = 2;
// getOwnPropertyDescriptor
// defineProperty
```

The `getOwnPropertyDescriptor(..)` and `defineProperty(..)` handlers are triggered by the default `set(..)` handler's steps when setting a property value (whether newly adding or updating). If you also define your own `set(..)` handler, you may or may not make the corresponding calls against `context` (not `target`!), which would trigger these proxy traps.

Proxy Limitations

These meta programming handlers trap a wide array of fundamental operations you can perform against an object. However, there are some operations that are not (yet, at least) available to intercept.

For example, none of these operations are trapped and forwarded from `pobj` proxy to `obj` target:

```
var obj = { a:1, b:2 },
    handlers = { .. },
    pobj = new Proxy( obj, handlers );

typeof obj;
String( obj );
obj + "";
obj == pobj;
obj === pobj
```

Perhaps in the future, more of these underlying fundamental operations in the language will be interceptable, giving us even more power to extend JavaScript from within itself.

There are certain *invariants*—behaviors that cannot be overridden—that apply to the use of proxy handlers. For example, the result from the `isExtensible(..)` handler is always coerced to a `boolean`. These invariants restrict some of your ability to customize behaviors with proxies, but they do so only to prevent you from creating strange and unusual (or inconsistent) behavior. The conditions for these invariants are complicated so we won't fully go into them here, but this post (*http://www.2ality.com/2014/12/es6-proxies.html#invariants*) does a great job of covering them.

Revocable Proxies

A regular proxy always traps for the target object, and cannot be modified after creation—as long as a reference is kept to the proxy, proxying remains possible. However, there may be cases where you want to create a proxy that can be disabled when you want to stop allowing it to proxy. The solution is to create a *revocable proxy*:

```
var obj = { a: 1 },
    handlers = {
        get(target,key,context) {
            // note: target === obj,
            // context === pobj
            console.log( "accessing: ", key );
            return target[key];
        }
    },
    { proxy: pobj, revoke: prevoke } =
        Proxy.revocable( obj, handlers );

pobj.a;
// accessing: a
// 1

// later:
prevoke();

pobj.a;
// TypeError
```

A revocable proxy is created with `Proxy.revocable(..)`, which is a regular function, not a constructor like `Proxy(..)`. Otherwise, it takes the same two arguments: *target* and *handlers*.

The return value of `Proxy.revocable(..)` is not the proxy itself as with `new Proxy(..)`. Instead, it's an object with two properties: *proxy* and *revoke*—we used object destructuring (see "Destructuring" on page 23 in Chapter 2) to assign these properties to `pobj` and `prevoke()` variables, respectively.

Once a revocable proxy is revoked, any attempts to access it (trigger any of its traps) will throw a `TypeError`.

An example of using a revocable proxy might be handing out a proxy to another party in your application that manages data in your model, instead of giving them a reference to the real model object itself. If your model object changes or is replaced, you want to invalidate the proxy you handed out so the other party knows (via the errors!) to request an updated reference to the model.

Using Proxies

The meta programming benefits of these Proxy handlers should be obvious. We can almost fully intercept (and thus override) the behavior of objects, meaning we can extend object behavior beyond core JS in some very powerful ways. We'll look at a few example patterns to explore the possibilities.

Proxy First, Proxy Last

As we mentioned earlier, you typically think of a proxy as "wrapping" the target object. In that sense, the proxy becomes the primary object the code interfaces with, and the actual target object remains hidden/protected.

You might do this because you want to pass the object somewhere that can't be fully "trusted," and so you need to enforce special rules around its access rather than passing the object itself.

Consider:

```
var messages = [],
    handlers = {
        get(target,key) {
            // string value?
            if (typeof target[key] == "string") {
                // filter out punctuation
                return target[key]
                    .replace( /[^\w]/g, "" );
            }
```

```
                // pass everything else through
                return target[key];
            },
            set(target,key,val) {
                // only set unique strings, lowercased
                if (typeof val == "string") {
                    val = val.toLowerCase();
                    if (target.indexOf( val ) == -1) {
                        target.push(
                            val.toLowerCase()
                        );
                    }
                }
                return true;
            }
        },
        messages_proxy =
            new Proxy( messages, handlers );

    // elsewhere:
    messages_proxy.push(
        "heLLo...", 42, "wOrlD!!", "WoRld!!"
    );

    messages_proxy.forEach( function(val){
        console.log(val);
    } );
    // hello world

    messages.forEach( function(val){
        console.log(val);
    } );
    // hello... world!!
```

I call this *proxy first* design, as we interact first (primarily, entirely) with the proxy.

We enforce some special rules on interacting with messages_proxy that aren't enforced for messages itself. We only add elements if the value is a string and is also unique; we also lowercase the value. When retrieving values from messages_proxy, we filter out any punctuation in the strings.

Alternatively, we can completely invert this pattern, where the target interacts with the proxy instead of the proxy interacting with the target. Thus, code really only interacts with the main object. The easiest way to accomplish this fallback is to have the proxy object in the [[Prototype]] chain of the main object.

Consider:

```
var handlers = {
        get(target,key,context) {
            return function() {
                context.speak(key + "!");
            };
        }
    },
    catchall = new Proxy( {}, handlers ),
    greeter = {
        speak(who = "someone") {
            console.log( "hello", who );
        }
    };

// set up `greeter` to fall back to `catchall`
Object.setPrototypeOf( greeter, catchall );

greeter.speak();              // hello someone
greeter.speak( "world" );     // hello world

greeter.everyone();           // hello everyone!
```

We interact directly with greeter instead of catchall. When we call speak(..), it's found on greeter and used directly. But when we try to access a method like everyone(), that function doesn't exist on greeter.

The default object property behavior is to check up the [[Prototype]] chain (see the *this & Object Prototypes* title of this series), so catchall is consulted for an everyone property. The proxy get() handler then kicks in and returns a function that calls speak(..) with the name of the property being accessed ("everyone").

I call this pattern *proxy last*, as the proxy is used only as a last resort.

"No Such Property/Method"

A common complaint about JS is that objects aren't by default very defensive in the situation where you try to access or set a property that doesn't already exist. You may wish to predefine all the properties/methods for an object, and have an error thrown if a nonexistent property name is subsequently used.

We can accomplish this with a proxy, either in *proxy first* or *proxy last* design. Let's consider both.

```
var obj = {
        a: 1,
        foo() {
            console.log( "a:", this.a );
        }
    },
    handlers = {
        get(target,key,context) {
            if (Reflect.has( target, key )) {
                return Reflect.get(
                    target, key, context
                );
            }
            else {
                throw "No such property/method!";
            }
        },
        set(target,key,val,context) {
            if (Reflect.has( target, key )) {
                return Reflect.set(
                    target, key, val, context
                );
            }
            else {
                throw "No such property/method!";
            }
        }
    },
    pobj = new Proxy( obj, handlers );

pobj.a = 3;
pobj.foo();             // a: 3

pobj.b = 4;             // Error: No such property/method!
pobj.bar();             // Error: No such property/method!
```

For both get(..) and set(..), we only forward the operation if the
target object's property already exists; an error is thrown otherwise.
The proxy object (pobj) is the main object code should interact
with, as it intercepts these actions to provide the protections.

Now, let's consider inverting with *proxy last* design:

```
var handlers = {
        get() {
            throw "No such property/method!";
        },
        set() {
            throw "No such property/method!";
        }
    },
```

```
pobj = new Proxy( {}, handlers ),
obj = {
    a: 1,
    foo() {
        console.log( "a:", this.a );
    }
};

// set up `obj` to fall back to `pobj`
Object.setPrototypeOf( obj, pobj );

obj.a = 3;
obj.foo();          // a: 3

obj.b = 4;          // Error: No such property/method!
obj.bar();          // Error: No such property/method!
```

The *proxy last* design here is a fair bit simpler with respect to how the handlers are defined. Instead of needing to intercept the [[Get]] and [[Set]] operations and only forward them if the target property exists, we instead rely on the fact that if either [[Get]] or [[Set]] get to our pobj fallback, the action has already traversed the whole [[Prototype]] chain and not found a matching property. We are free at that point to unconditionally throw the error. Cool, huh?

Proxy Hacking the [[Prototype]] Chain

The [[Get]] operation is the primary channel by which the [[Proto type]] mechanism is invoked. When a property is not found on the immediate object, [[Get]] automatically hands off the operation to the [[Prototype]] object.

That means you can use the get(..) trap of a proxy to emulate or extend the notion of this [[Prototype]] mechanism.

The first hack we'll consider is creating two objects that are circularly linked via [[Prototype]] (or, at least it appears that way!). You cannot actually create a real circular [[Prototype]] chain, as the engine will throw an error. But a proxy can fake it!

Consider:

```
var handlers = {
    get(target,key,context) {
        if (Reflect.has( target, key )) {
            return Reflect.get(
                target, key, context
```

```
            );
        }
        // fake circular `[[Prototype]]`
        else {
            return Reflect.get(
                target[
                    Symbol.for( "[[Prototype]]" )
                ],
                key,
                context
            );
        }
    }
},
obj1 = new Proxy(
    {
        name: "obj-1",
        foo() {
            console.log( "foo:", this.name );
        }
    },
    handlers
),
obj2 = Object.assign(
    Object.create( obj1 ),
    {
        name: "obj-2",
        bar() {
            console.log( "bar:", this.name );
            this.foo();
        }
    }
);

// fake circular `[[Prototype]]` link
obj1[ Symbol.for( "[[Prototype]]" ) ] = obj2;

obj1.bar();
// bar: obj-1 <-- through proxy faking [[Prototype]]
// foo: obj-1 <-- `this` context still preserved

obj2.foo();
// foo: obj-2 <-- through [[Prototype]]
```

We didn't need to proxy/forward [[Set]] in this example, so we kept things simpler. To be fully [[Prototype]] emulation compliant, you'd want to implement a set(..) handler that searches the [[Prototype]] chain for a matching property and respects its descriptor behavior (e.g., set, writable). See the *this & Object Prototypes* title of this series.

In the previous snippet, obj2 is [[Prototype]] linked to obj1 by virtue of the Object.create(..) statement. But to create the reverse (circular) linkage, we create property on obj1 at the symbol location Symbol.for("[[Prototype]]") (see "Symbols" on page 80 in Chapter 2). This symbol may look sort of special/magical, but it isn't. It just allows me a conveniently named hook that semantically appears related to the task I'm performing.

Then, the proxy's get(..) handler looks first to see if a requested key is on the proxy. If not, the operation is manually handed off to the object reference stored in the Symbol.for("[[Prototype]]") location of target.

One important advantage of this pattern is that the definitions of obj1 and obj2 are mostly not intruded by the setting up of this circular relationship between them. Although the previous snippet has all the steps intertwined for brevity's sake, if you look closely, the proxy handler logic is entirely generic (doesn't know about obj1 or obj2 specifically). So, that logic could be pulled out into a simple helper that wires them up, like a setCircularPrototypeOf(..) for example. We'll leave that as an exercise for the reader.

Now that we've seen how we can use get(..) to emulate a [[Proto type]] link, let's push the hackery a bit further. Instead of a circular [[Prototype]], what about multiple [[Prototype]] linkages (aka "multiple inheritance")? This turns out to be fairly straightforward:

```
var obj1 = {
    name: "obj-1",
    foo() {
        console.log( "obj1.foo:", this.name );
    },
},
obj2 = {
    name: "obj-2",
    foo() {
```

```
                console.log( "obj2.foo:", this.name );
            },
            bar() {
                console.log( "obj2.bar:", this.name );
            }
        },
        handlers = {
            get(target,key,context) {
                if (Reflect.has( target, key )) {
                    return Reflect.get(
                        target, key, context
                    );
                }
                // fake multiple `[[Prototype]]`
                else {
                    for (var P of target[
                        Symbol.for( "[[Prototype]]" )
                    ]) {
                        if (Reflect.has( P, key )) {
                            return Reflect.get(
                                P, key, context
                            );
                        }
                    }
                }
            }
        },
        obj3 = new Proxy(
            {
                name: "obj-3",
                baz() {
                    this.foo();
                    this.bar();
                }
            },
            handlers
        );

// fake multiple `[[Prototype]]` links
obj3[ Symbol.for( "[[Prototype]]" ) ] = [
    obj1, obj2
];

obj3.baz();
// obj1.foo: obj-3
// obj2.bar: obj-3
```

As mentioned in the note after the earlier circular [[Prototype]] example, we didn't implement the set(..) handler, but it would be necessary for a complete solution that emulates [[Set]] actions as normal [[Prototype]]s behave.

obj3 is set up to multiple-delegate to both obj1 and obj2. In obj3.baz(), the this.foo() call ends up pulling foo() from obj1 (first-come, first-served, even though there's also a foo() on obj2). If we reordered the linkage as obj2, obj1, the obj2.foo() would have been found and used.

But as is, the this.bar() call doesn't find a bar() on obj1, so it falls over to check obj2, where it finds a match.

obj1 and obj2 represent two parallel [[Prototype]] chains of obj3. obj1 and/or obj2 could themselves have normal [[Prototype]] delegation to other objects, or either could themself be a proxy (like obj3 is) that can multiple-delegate.

Just as with the circular [[Prototype]] example earlier, the definitions of obj1, obj2, and obj3 are almost entirely separate from the generic proxy logic that handles the multiple-delegation. It would be trivial to define a utility like setPrototypesOf(..) (notice the "s"!) that takes a main object and a list of objects to fake the multiple [[Prototype]] linkage to. Again, we'll leave that as an exercise for the reader.

Hopefully the power of proxies is now becoming clearer after these various examples. There are many other powerful meta programming tasks that proxies enable.

Reflect API

The Reflect object is a plain object (like Math), not a function/ constructor like the other built-in natives.

It holds static functions that correspond to various meta programming tasks you can control. These functions correspond one-to-one with the handler methods (*traps*) that proxies can define.

Some of the functions will look familiar as functions of the same names on Object:

- `Reflect.getOwnPropertyDescriptor(..)`

- `Reflect.defineProperty(..)`

- `Reflect.getPrototypeOf(..)`

- `Reflect.setPrototypeOf(..)`

- `Reflect.preventExtensions(..)`

- `Reflect.isExtensible(..)`

These utilities in general behave the same as their `Object.*` counterparts. However, one difference is that the `Object.*` counterparts attempt to coerce their first argument (the target object) to an object if it's not already one. The `Reflect.*` methods simply throw an error in that case.

An object's keys can be accessed/inspected using these utilities:

`Reflect.ownKeys(..)`
> Returns the list of all owned keys (not "inherited"), as returned by both `Object.getOwnPropertyNames(..)` and `Object.getOwnPropertySymbols(..)`. See "Property Ordering" on page 226 for information about the order of keys.

`Reflect.enumerate(..)`
> Returns an iterator that produces the set of all nonsymbol keys (owned and "inherited") that are *enumerable* (see the *this & Object Prototypes* title of this series). Essentially, this set of keys is the same as those processed by a `for..in` loop. See "Property Ordering" on page 226 for information about the order of keys.

`Reflect.has(..)`
> Essentially the same as the `in` operator for checking if a property is on an object or its `[[Prototype]]` chain. For example, `Reflect.has(o,"foo")` essentially performs `"foo" in o`.

Function calls and constructor invocations can be performed manually, separate of the normal syntax (e.g., `(..)` and `new`) using these utilities:

`Reflect.apply(..)`
> For example, `Reflect.apply(foo,thisObj,[42,"bar"])` calls the `foo(..)` function with `thisObj` as its `this`, and passes in the 42 and `"bar"` arguments.

```
Reflect.construct(..)
```
For example, `Reflect.construct(foo,[42,"bar"])` essentially calls `new foo(42,"bar")`.

Object property access, setting, and deletion can be performed manually using these utilities:

```
Reflect.get(..)
```
For example, `Reflect.get(o,"foo")` retrieves `o.foo`.

```
Reflect.set(..)
```
For example, `Reflect.set(o,"foo",42)` essentially performs `o.foo = 42`.

```
Reflect.deleteProperty(..)
```
For example, `Reflect.deleteProperty(o,"foo")` essentially performs `delete o.foo`.

The meta programming capabilities of `Reflect` give you programmatic equivalents to emulate various syntactic features, exposing previously hidden-only abstract operations. For example, you can use these capabilities to extend features and APIs for *domain specific languages* (DSLs).

Property Ordering

Prior to ES6, the order used to list an object's keys/properties was implementation dependent and undefined by the specification. Generally, most engines have enumerated them in creation order, though developers have been strongly encouraged not to ever rely on this ordering.

As of ES6, the order for listing owned properties is now defined (ES6 specification, section 9.1.12) by the `[[OwnPropertyKeys]]` algorithm, which produces all owned properties (strings or symbols), regardless of enumerability. This ordering is only guaranteed for `Reflect.ownKeys(..)` (and by extension, `Object.getOwnProper tyNames(..)` and `Object.getOwnPropertySymbols(..)`).

The ordering is:

1. First, enumerate any owned properties that are integer indexes, in ascending numeric order.

---

2. Next, enumerate the rest of the owned string property names in creation order.

3. Finally, enumerate owned symbol properties in creation order.

Consider:

```
var o = {};

o[Symbol("c")] = "yay";
o[2] = true;
o[1] = true;
o.b = "awesome";
o.a = "cool";

Reflect.ownKeys( o );              // [1,2,"b","a",Symbol(c)]
Object.getOwnPropertyNames( o );   // [1,2,"b","a"]
Object.getOwnPropertySymbols( o ); // [Symbol(c)]
```

On the other hand, the [[Enumerate]] algorithm (ES6 specification, section 9.1.11) produces only enumerable properties, from the target object as well as its [[Prototype]] chain. It is used by both Reflect.enumerate(..) and for..in. The observable ordering is implementation dependent and not controlled by the specification.

By contrast, Object.keys(..) invokes the [[OwnPropertyKeys]] algorithm to get a list of all owned keys. However, it filters out non-enumerable properties and then reorders the list to match legacy implementation-dependent behavior, specifically with JSON.string ify(..) and for..in. So, by extension the ordering *also* matches that of Reflect.enumerate(..).

In other words, all four mechanisms (Reflect.enumerate(..), Object.keys(..), for..in, and JSON.stringify(..)) will match with the same implementation-dependent ordering, though they technically get there in different ways.

Implementations are allowed to match these four to the ordering of [[OwnPropertyKeys]], but are not required to. Nevertheless, you will likely observe the following ordering behavior from them:

```
var o = { a: 1, b: 2 };
var p = Object.create( o );
p.c = 3;
p.d = 4;

for (var prop of Reflect.enumerate( p )) {
    console.log( prop );
```

```
}
// c d a b

for (var prop in p) {
    console.log( prop );
}
// c d a b

JSON.stringify( p );
// {"c":3,"d":4}

Object.keys( p );
// ["c","d"]
```

Boiling this all down: as of ES6, `Reflect.ownKeys(..)`, `Object.getOwnPropertyNames(..)`, and `Object.getOwnProperty` `Symbols(..)` all have predictable and reliable ordering guaranteed by the specification. So it's safe to build code that relies on this ordering.

`Reflect.enumerate(..)`, `Object.keys(..)`, and `for..in` (as well as `JSON.stringification(..)` by extension) continue to share an observable ordering with each other, as they always have. But that ordering will not necessarily be the same as that of `Reflect.own` `Keys(..)`. Care should still be taken in relying on their implementation-dependent ordering.

Feature Testing

What is a feature test? It's a test you run to determine if a feature is available or not. Sometimes, the test is not just for existence, but for conformance to specified behavior—features can exist but be buggy.

This is a meta programming technique, to test the environment your program runs in to then determine how your program should behave.

The most common use of feature tests in JS is checking for the existence of an API and if it's not present, defining a polyfill (see Chapter 1). For example:

```
if (!Number.isNaN) {
    Number.isNaN = function(x) {
        return x !== x;
    };
}
```

The if statement in this snippet is meta programming: we're prob-ing our program and its runtime environment to determine if and how we should proceed.

But what about testing for features that involve new syntax?

You might try something like:

```
try {
    a = () => {};
    ARROW_FUNCS_ENABLED = true;
}
catch (err) {
    ARROW_FUNCS_ENABLED = false;
}
```

Unfortunately, this doesn't work, because our JS programs are com-piled. Thus, the engine will choke on the () => {} syntax if it is not already supporting ES6 arrow functions. Having a syntax error in your program prevents it from running, which prevents your pro-gram from subsequently responding differently if the feature is sup-ported or not.

To meta program with feature tests around syntax-related features, we need a way to insulate the test from the initial compile step our program runs through. For instance, if we could store the code for the test in a string, then the JS engine wouldn't by default try to compile the contents of that string, until we asked it to.

Did your mind just jump to using eval(..)?

Not so fast. See the *Scope & Closures* title of this series for why eval(..) is a bad idea. But there's another option with less down-sides: the Function(..) constructor.

Consider:

```
try {
    new Function( "( () => {} )" );
    ARROW_FUNCS_ENABLED = true;
}
catch (err) {
    ARROW_FUNCS_ENABLED = false;
}
```

OK, so now we're meta programming by determining if a feature like arrow functions *can* compile in the current engine or not. You might then wonder, what would we do with this information?

With existence checks for APIs, and defining fallback API polyfills, there's a clear path for what to do with either test success or failure. But what can we do with the information we get from ARROW_FUNCS_ENABLED being `true` or `false`?

Because the syntax can't appear in a file if the engine doesn't support that feature, you can't just have different functions defined in the file with and without the syntax in question.

What you can do is use the test to determine which of a set of JS files you should load. For example, if you had a set of these feature tests in a bootstrapper for your JS application, it could then test the environment to determine if your ES6 code can be loaded and run directly, or if you need to load a transpiled version of your code (see Chapter 1).

This technique is called *split delivery*.

It recognizes the reality that your ES6 authored JS programs will sometimes be able to entirely run "natively" in ES6+ browsers, but other times need transpilation to run in pre-ES6 browsers. If you always load and use the transpiled code, even in the new ES6-compliant environments, you're running suboptimal code at least some of the time. This is not ideal.

Split delivery is more complicated and sophisticated, but it represents a more mature and robust approach to bridging the gap between the code you write and the feature support in browsers your programs must run in.

FeatureTests.io

Defining feature tests for all of the ES6+ syntax, as well as the semantic behaviors, is a daunting task you probably don't want to tackle yourself. Because these tests require dynamic compilation (`new Function(..)`), there's some unfortunate performance cost.

Moreover, running these tests every single time your app runs is probably wasteful, as on average a user's browser only updates once in a several week period at most, and even then, new features aren't necessarily showing up with every update.

Finally, managing the list of feature tests that apply to your specific code base—rarely will your programs use the entirety of ES6—is unruly and error-prone.

FeatureTests.io (*https://featuretests.io*) offers solutions to these frustrations.

You can load the service's library into your page, and it loads the latest test definitions and runs all the feature tests. It does so using background processing with Web Workers, if possible, to reduce the performance overhead. It also uses LocalStorage persistence to cache the results in a way that can be shared across all sites you visit which use the service, which drastically reduces how often the tests need to run on each browser instance.

You get runtime feature tests in each of your users' browsers, and you can use those tests results dynamically to serve users the most appropriate code (no more, no less) for their environments.

Moreover, the service provides tools and APIs to scan your files to determine what features you need, so you can fully automate your split delivery build processes.

FeatureTests.io makes it practical to use feature tests for all parts of ES6 and beyond to make sure that only the best code is ever loaded and run for any given environment.

Tail Call Optimization (TCO)

Normally, when a function call is made from inside another function, a second *stack frame* is allocated to separately manage the variables/state of that other function invocation. Not only does this allocation cost some processing time, but it also takes up some extra memory.

A call stack chain typically has at most 10-15 jumps from one function to another and another. In those scenarios, the memory usage is not likely any kind of practical problem.

However, when you consider recursive programming (a function calling itself repeatedly)—or mutual recursion with two or more functions calling each other—the call stack could easily be hundreds, thousands, or more levels deep. You can probably see the problems that could cause, if memory usage grows unbounded.

JavaScript engines have to set an arbitrary limit to prevent such programming techniques from crashing by running the browser and device out of memory. That's why we get the frustrating "RangeError: Maximum call stack size exceeded" thrown if the limit is hit.

The limit of call stack depth is not controlled by the specification. It's implementation dependent, and will vary between browsers and devices. You should never code with strong assumptions of exact observable limits, as they may very well change from release to release.

Certain patterns of function calls, called *tail calls*, can be optimized in a way to avoid the extra allocation of stack frames. If the extra allocation can be avoided, there's no reason to arbitrarily limit the call stack depth, so the engines can let them run unbounded.

A tail call is a `return` statement with a function call, where nothing has to happen after the call except returning its value.

This optimization can only be applied in `strict` mode. Yet another reason to always write all your code as `strict`!

Here's a function call that is *not* in tail position:

```
"use strict";

function foo(x) {
    return x * 2;
}

function bar(x) {
    // not a tail call
    return 1 + foo( x );
}

bar( 10 );              // 21
```

`1 + ..` has to be performed after the `foo(x)` call completes, so the state of that `bar(..)` invocation needs to be preserved.

But the following snippet demonstrates calls to `foo(..)` and `bar(..)` where both *are* in tail position, as they're the last thing to happen in their code path (other than the `return`):

```
"use strict";

function foo(x) {
    return x * 2;
}

function bar(x) {
    x = x + 1;
    if (x > 10) {
```

```
        return foo( x );
    }
    else {
        return bar( x + 1 );
    }
}

bar( 5 );                   // 24
bar( 15 );                  // 32
```

In this program, bar(..) is clearly recursive, but foo(..) is just a regular function call. In both cases, the function calls are in *proper tail position*. The x + 1 is evaluated before the bar(..) call, and whenever that call finishes, all that happens is the return.

Proper Tail Calls (PTC) of these forms can be optimized—called Tail Call Optimization (TCO)—so that the extra stack frame allocation is unnecessary. Instead of creating a new stack frame for the next function call, the engine just reuses the existing stack frame. That works because a function doesn't need to preserve any of the current state, as nothing happens with that state after the PTC.

TCO means there's practically no limit to how deep the call stack can be. That trick slightly improves regular function calls in normal programs, but more importantly opens the door to using recursion for program expression even if the call stack could be tens of thousands of calls deep.

We're no longer relegated to simply theorizing about recursion for problem solving, but can actually use it in real JavaScript programs!

As of ES6, all PTC should be optimizable in this way, recursion or not.

Tail Call Rewrite

The hitch, however, is that only PTC can be optimized; non-PTC will still work of course, but will cause stack frame allocation as they always did. You'll have to be careful about structuring your functions with PTC if you expect the optimizations to kick in.

If you have a function that's not written with PTC, you may find the need to manually rearrange your code to be eligible for TCO.

Consider:

```
"use strict";
```

```
function foo(x) {
    if (x <= 1) return 1;
    return (x / 2) + foo( x - 1 );
}

foo( 123456 );              // RangeError
```

The call to foo(x-1) isn't a PTC because its result has to be added to
(x / 2) before returning.

However, to make this code eligible for TCO in an ES6 engine, we
can rewrite it as follows:

```
"use strict";

var foo = (function(){
    function _foo(acc,x) {
        if (x <= 1) return acc;
        return _foo( (x / 2) + acc, x - 1 );
    }

    return function(x) {
        return _foo( 1, x );
    };
})();

foo( 123456 );              // 3810376848.5
```

If you run the previous snippet in an ES6 engine that implements
TCO, you'll get the 3810376848.5 answer as shown. However, it'll
still fail with a RangeError in non-TCO engines.

Non-TCO Optimizations

There are other techniques to rewrite the code so that the call stack
isn't growing with each call.

One such technique is called *trampolining*, which amounts to having
each partial result represented as a function that either returns
another partial result function or the final result. Then you can simply loop until you stop getting a function, and you'll have the result.
Consider:

```
"use strict";

function trampoline( res ) {
    while (typeof res == "function") {
        res = res();
    }
    return res;
```

```
    }

    var foo = (function(){
        function _foo(acc,x) {
            if (x <= 1) return acc;
            return function partial(){
                return _foo( (x / 2) + acc, x - 1 );
            };
        }

        return function(x) {
            return trampoline( _foo( 1, x ) );
        };
    })();

    foo( 123456 );            // 3810376848.5
```

This reworking required minimal changes to factor out the recursion into the loop in `trampoline(..)`:

1. First, we wrapped the `return _foo ..` line in the `return partial() { ..` function expression.

2. Then we wrapped the `_foo(1,x)` call in the `trampoline(..)` call.

The reason this technique doesn't suffer the call stack limitation is that each of those inner `partial(..)` functions is just returned back to the `while` loop in `trampoline(..)`, which runs it and then loop iterates again. In other words, `partial(..)` doesn't recursively call itself, it just returns another function. The stack depth remains constant, so it can run as long as it needs to.

Trampolining expressed in this way uses the closure that the inner `partial()` function has over the `x` and `acc` variables to keep the state from iteration to iteration. The advantage is that the looping logic is pulled out into a reusable `trampoline(..)` utility function, which many libraries provide versions of. You can reuse `trampoline(..)` multiple times in your program with different trampolined algorithms.

Of course, if you really wanted to deeply optimize (and the reusability wasn't a concern), you could discard the closure state and inline the state tracking of `acc` into just one function's scope along with a loop. This technique is generally called *recursion unrolling*:

```
"use strict";

function foo(x) {
    var acc = 1;
    while (x > 1) {
        acc = (x / 2) + acc;
        x = x - 1;
    }
    return acc;
}

foo( 123456 );          // 3810376848.5
```

This expression of the algorithm is simpler to read, and will likely perform the best (strictly speaking) of the various forms we've explored. That may seem like a clear winner, and you may wonder why you would ever try the other approaches.

There are some reasons why you might not want to always manually unroll your recursions:

- Instead of factoring out the trampolining (loop) logic for reusability, we've inlined it. This works great when there's only one example to consider, but as soon as you have a half dozen or more of these in your program, there's a good chance you'll want some reusability to keep things shorter and more manageable.

- The example here is deliberately simple enough to illustrate the different forms. In practice, there are many more complications in recursion algorithms, such as mutual recursion (more than just one function calling itself).

The farther you go down this rabbit hole, the more manual and intricate the *unrolling* optimizations are. You'll quickly lose all the perceived value of readability. The primary advantage of recursion, even in the PTC form, is that it preserves the algorithm readability, and offloads the performance optimization to the engine.

If you write your algorithms with PTC, the ES6 engine will apply TCO to let your code run in constant stack depth (by reusing stack frames). You get the readability of recursion with most of the performance benefits and no limitations of run length.

Meta?

What does TCO have to do with meta programming?

As we covered in "Feature Testing" on page 228 earlier, you can determine at runtime what features an engine supports. This includes TCO, though determining it is quite brute force. Consider:

```
"use strict";

try {
    (function foo(x){
        if (x < 5E5) return foo( x + 1 );
    })( 1 );

    TCO_ENABLED = true;
}
catch (err) {
    TCO_ENABLED = false;
}
```

In a non-TCO engine, the recursive loop will fail out eventually, throwing an exception caught by the try..catch. Otherwise, the loop completes easily thanks to TCO.

Yuck, right?

But how could meta programming around the TCO feature (or rather, the lack thereof) benefit our code? The simple answer is that you could use such a feature test to decide to load a version of your application's code that uses recursion, or an alternative one that's been converted/transpiled to not need recursion.

Self-Adjusting Code

But here's another way of looking at the problem:

```
"use strict";

function foo(x) {
    function _foo() {
        if (x > 1) {
            acc = acc + (x / 2);
            x = x - 1;
            return _foo();
        }
    }

    var acc = 1;

    while (x > 1) {
        try {
            _foo();
        }
```

```
        catch (err) { }
    }

    return acc;
}

foo( 123456 );          // 3810376848.5
```

This algorithm works by attempting to do as much of the work with recursion as possible, but keeping track of the progress via scoped variables x and acc. If the entire problem can be solved with recursion without an error, great. If the engine kills the recursion at some point, we simply catch that with the try..catch and then try again, picking up where we left off.

I consider this a form of meta programming in that you are probing during runtime the ability of the engine to fully (recursively) finish the task, and working around any (non-TCO) engine limitations that may restrict you.

At first (or even second!) glance, my bet is this code seems much uglier to you compared to some of the earlier versions. It also runs a fair bit slower (on larger runs in a non-TCO environment).

The primary advantage, other than it being able to complete any size task even in non-TCO engines, is that this "solution" to the recursion stack limitation is much more flexible than the trampolining or manual unrolling techniques shown previously.

Essentially, _foo() in this case is a sort of stand-in for practically any recursive task, even mutual recursion. The rest is the boilerplate that should work for just about any algorithm.

The only "catch" is that to be able to resume in the event of a recursion limit being hit, the state of the recursion must be in scoped variables that exist outside the recursive function(s). We did that by leaving x and acc outside of the _foo() function, instead of passing them as arguments to _foo() as earlier.

Almost any recursive algorithm can be adapted to work this way. That means it's the most widely applicable way of leveraging TCO with recursion in your programs, with minimal rewriting.

This approach still uses a PTC, meaning this code will *progressively enhance* from running using the loop many times (recursion batches) in an older browser to fully leveraging TCO'd recursion in an ES6+ environment. I think that's pretty cool!

Review

Meta programming is when you turn the logic of your program to focus on itself (or its runtime environment), either to inspect its own structure or to modify it. The primary value of meta programming is to extend the normal mechanisms of the language to provide additional capabilities.

Prior to ES6, JavaScript already had quite a bit of meta programming capability, but ES6 significantly ramps that up with several new features.

From function name inferences for anonymous functions to meta properties that give you information about things like how a constructor was invoked, you can inspect the program structure while it runs more than ever before. Well-Known Symbols let you override intrinsic behaviors, such as coercion of an object to a primitive value. Proxies can intercept and customize various low-level operations on objects, and `Reflect` provides utilities to emulate them.

Feature testing, even for subtle semantic behaviors like Tail Call Optimization, shifts the meta programming focus from your program to the JS engine capabilities itself. By knowing more about what the environment can do, your programs can adjust themselves to the best fit as they run.

Should you meta program? My advice is: first focus on learning how the core mechanics of the language really work. But once you fully know what JS itself can do, it's time to start leveraging these powerful meta programming capabilities to push the language further!

CHAPTER 8

Beyond ES6

At the time of this writing, the final draft of ES6 (*ECMAScript 2015*) is shortly headed toward its final official vote of approval by ECMA. But even as ES6 is being finalized, the TC39 committee is already hard at work at on features for ES7/2016 and beyond.

As we discussed in Chapter 1, it's expected that the cadence of progress for JS is going to accelerate from updating once every several years to having an official version update once per year (hence the year-based naming). That alone is going to radically change how JS developers learn about and keep up with the language.

But even more importantly, the committee is actually going to work feature by feature. As soon as a feature is spec-complete and has its kinks worked out through implementation experiments in a few browsers, that feature will be considered stable enough to start using. We're all strongly encouraged to adopt features once they're ready instead of waiting for some official standards vote. If you haven't already learned ES6, the time is *past due* to get on board!

As the time of this writing, a list of future proposals and their status can be seen here (*https://github.com/tc39/ecma262#current-proposals*).

Transpilers and polyfills are how we'll bridge to these new features even before all browsers we support have implemented them. Babel, Traceur, and several other major transpilers already have support for some of the post-ES6 features that are most likely to stabilize.

With that in mind, it's already time for us to look at some of them. Let's jump in!

 These features are all in various stages of development. While they're likely to land, and probably will look similar, take the contents of this chapter with more than a few grains of salt. This chapter will evolve in future editions of this title as these (and other!) features finalize.

async functions

In "Generators + Promises" on page 155 in Chapter 4, we mentioned that there's a proposal for direct syntactic support for the pattern of generators yielding promises to a runner-like utility that will resume it on promise completion. Let's take a brief look at that proposed feature, called async function.

Recall this generator example from Chapter 4:

```
run( function *main() {
    var ret = yield step1();

    try {
        ret = yield step2( ret );
    }
    catch (err) {
        ret = yield step2Failed( err );
    }

    ret = yield Promise.all([
        step3a( ret ),
        step3b( ret ),
        step3c( ret )
    ]);

    yield step4( ret );
} )
.then(
    function fulfilled(){
        // `*main()` completed successfully
    },
    function rejected(reason){
        // Oops, something went wrong
    }
);
```

The proposed `async function` syntax can express this same flow control logic without needing the `run(..)` utility, because JS will automatically know how to look for promises to wait and resume. Consider:

```
async function main() {
    var ret = await step1();

    try {
        ret = await step2( ret );
    }
    catch (err) {
        ret = await step2Failed( err );
    }

    ret = await Promise.all( [
        step3a( ret ),
        step3b( ret ),
        step3c( ret )
    ] );

    await step4( ret );
}

main()
.then(
    function fulfilled(){
        // `main()` completed successfully
    },
    function rejected(reason){
        // Oops, something went wrong
    }
);
```

Instead of the `function *main() { ..` declaration, we declare with the `async function main() { ..` form. And instead of yielding a promise, we `await` the promise. The call to run the function `main()` actually returns a promise that we can directly observe. That's the equivalent to the promise we get back from a `run(main)` call.

Do you see the symmetry? `async function` is essentially syntactic sugar for the generators + promises + `run(..)` pattern; under the covers, it operates the same!

If you're a C# developer and this async/await looks familiar, it's because this feature is directly inspired by C#'s feature. It's nice to see language precedence informing convergence!

Babel, Traceur, and other transpilers already have early support for the current status of `async functions`, so you can start using them already. However, in the next section, we'll see why you perhaps shouldn't jump on that ship quite yet.

 There's also a proposal for `async function*`, which would be called an "async generator." You can both `yield` and `await` in the same code, and even combine those operations in the same statement: `x = await yield y`. The "async generator" proposal seems to be more in flux—namely, its return value is not fully worked out yet. Some feel it should be an *observable*, which is kind of like the combination of an iterator and a promise. For now, we won't go further into that topic, but stay tuned as it evolves.

Caveats

One unresolved point of contention with `async function` is that because it only returns a promise, there's no way from the outside to *cancel* an `async function` instance that's currently running. This can be a problem if the async operation is resource-intensive, and you want to free up the resources as soon as you're sure the result won't be needed.

For example:

```
async function request(url) {
    var resp = await (
        new Promise( function(resolve,reject){
            var xhr = new XMLHttpRequest();
            xhr.open( "GET", url );
            xhr.onreadystatechange = function(){
                if (xhr.readyState == 4) {
                    if (xhr.status == 200) {
                        resolve( xhr );
                    }
                    else {
                        reject( xhr.statusText );
                    }
                }
            };
            xhr.send();
        } )
    );
```

```
        return resp.responseText;
    }

    var pr = request( "http://some.url.1" );

    pr.then(
        function fulfilled(responseText){
            // ajax success
        },
        function rejected(reason){
            // Oops, something went wrong
        }
    );
```

This `request(..)` that I've conceived is somewhat like the `fetch(..)` utility that's recently been proposed for inclusion into the web platform. So the concern is, what happens if you want to use the `pr` value to somehow indicate that you want to cancel a long-running Ajax request, for example?

Promises are not cancelable (at the time of writing, anyway). In my opinion, as well as many others, they never should be (see the *Async & Performance* title of this series). And even if a promise did have a `cancel()` method on it, does that necessarily mean that calling `pr.cancel()` should actually propagate a cancelation signal all the way back up the promise chain to the `async function`?

Several possible resolutions to this debate have surfaced:

- `async functions` won't be cancelable at all (status quo)
- A "cancel token" can be passed to an async function at call time
- Return value changes to a cancelable-promise type that's added
- Return value changes to something else nonpromise (e.g., observable, or control token with promise and cancel capabilities)

At the time of this writing, `async functions` return regular promises, so it's less likely that the return value will entirely change. But it's too early to tell where things will land. Keep an eye on this discussion.

Object.observe(..)

One of the holy grails of front-end web development is data binding —listening for updates to a data object and syncing the DOM representation of that data. Most JS frameworks provide some mechanism for these sorts of operations.

It appears likely that post-ES6, we'll see support added directly to the language, via a utility called `Object.observe(..)`. Essentially, the idea is that you can set up a listener to observe an object's changes, and have a callback called any time a change occurs. You can then update the DOM accordingly, for instance.

There are six types of changes that you can observe:

- add
- update
- delete
- reconfigure
- setPrototype
- preventExtensions

By default, you'll be notified of all these change types, but you can filter down to only the ones you care about.

Consider:

```
var obj = { a: 1, b: 2 };

Object.observe(
    obj,
    function(changes){
        for (var change of changes) {
            console.log( change );
        }
    },
    [ "add", "update", "delete" ]
);

obj.c = 3;
// { name: "c", object: obj, type: "add" }

obj.a = 42;
// { name: "a", object: obj, type: "update", oldValue: 1 }
```

```
delete obj.b;
// { name: "b", object: obj, type: "delete", oldValue: 2 }
```

In addition to the main "add", "update", and "delete" change types:

- The "reconfigure" change event is fired if one of the object's properties is reconfigured with Object.defineProperty(..), such as changing its writable attribute. See the *this & Object Prototypes* title of this series for more information.

- The "preventExtensions" change event is fired if the object is made non-extensible via Object.preventExtensions(..).

Because both Object.seal(..) and Object.freeze(..) also imply Object.preventExtensions(..), they'll also fire its corresponding change event. In addition, "reconfigure" change events will also be fired for each property on the object. * The "setPrototype" change event is fired if the [[Prototype]] of an object is changed, either by setting it with the __proto__ setter, or using Object.setPrototy peOf(..).

Notice that these change events are notified immediately after said change. Don't confuse this with proxies (see Chapter 7) where you can intercept the actions before they occur. Object observation lets you respond after a change (or set of changes) occurs.

Custom Change Events

In addition to the six built-in change event types, you can also listen for and fire custom change events.

Consider:

```
function observer(changes){
    for (var change of changes) {
        if (change.type == "recalc") {
            change.object.c =
                change.object.oldValue +
                change.object.a +
                change.object.b;
        }
    }
}

function changeObj(a,b) {
    var notifier = Object.getNotifier( obj );
```

```
    obj.a = a * 2;
    obj.b = b * 3;

    // queue up change events into a set
    notifier.notify( {
        type: "recalc",
        name: "c",
        oldValue: obj.c
    } );
}

var obj = { a: 1, b: 2, c: 3 };

Object.observe(
    obj,
    observer,
    ["recalc"]
);

changeObj( 3, 11 );

obj.a;          // 12
obj.b;          // 30
obj.c;          // 3
```

The change set ("recalc" custom event) has been queued for delivery to the observer, but not delivered yet, which is why obj.c is still 3.

The changes are by default delivered at the end of the current event loop (see the *Async & Performance* title of this series). If you want to deliver them immediately, use Object.deliverChangeRecords(observer). Once the change events are delivered, you can observe obj.c updated as expected:

```
obj.c;          // 42
```

In the previous example, we called notifier.notify(..) with the complete change event record. An alternative form for queuing change records is to use performChange(..), which separates specifying the type of the event from the rest of event record's properties (via a function callback). Consider:

```
notifier.performChange( "recalc", function(){
    return {
        name: "c",
        // `this` is the object under observation
        oldValue: this.c
```

```
        };
    } );
```

In certain circumstances, this separation of concerns may map more cleanly to your usage pattern.

Ending Observation

Just like with normal event listeners, you may wish to stop observing an object's change events. For that, you use `Object.unobserve(..)`.

For example:

```
var obj = { a: 1, b: 2 };

Object.observe( obj, function observer(changes) {
    for (var change of changes) {
        if (change.type == "setPrototype") {
            Object.unobserve(
                change.object, observer
            );
            break;
        }
    }
} );
```

In this trivial example, we listen for change events until we see the `"setPrototype"` event come through, at which time we stop observing any more change events.

Exponentiation Operator

An operator has been proposed for JavaScript to perform exponentiation in the same way that `Math.pow(..)` does. Consider:

```
var a = 2;

a ** 4;        // Math.pow( a, 4 ) == 16

a **= 3;       // a = Math.pow( a, 3 )
a;             // 8
```

 `**` is essentially the same as it appears in Python, Ruby, Perl, and others.

Objects Properties and . . .

As we saw in "Too Many, Too Few, Just Enough" on page 30 in Chapter 2, the . . . operator is pretty obvious in how it relates to spreading or gathering arrays. But what about objects?

Such a feature was considered for ES6, but was deferred to be considered after ES6 (aka "ES7" or "ES2016" or ...). Here's how it might work in that "beyond ES6" timeframe:

```
var o1 = { a: 1, b: 2 },
    o2 = { c: 3 },
    o3 = { ...o1, ...o2, d: 4 };

console.log( o3.a, o3.b, o3.c, o3.d );
// 1 2 3 4
```

The . . . operator might also be used to gather an object's destructured properties back into an object:

```
var o1 = { b: 2, c: 3, d: 4 };
var { b, ...o2 } = o1;

console.log( b, o2.c, o2.d );       // 2 3 4
```

Here, the . . .o2 re-gathers the destructured c and d properties back into an o2 object (o2 does not have a b property like o1 does).

Again, these are just proposals under consideration beyond ES6. But it'll be cool if they do land.

Array#includes(..)

One extremely common task JS developers need to perform is searching for a value inside an array of values. The way this has always been done is:

```
var vals = [ "foo", "bar", 42, "baz" ];

if (vals.indexOf( 42 ) >= 0) {
    // found it!
}
```

The reason for the >= 0 check is because indexOf(..) returns a numeric value of 0 or greater if found, or -1 if not found. In other words, we're using an index-returning function in a boolean context. But because -1 is truthy instead of falsy, we have to be more manual with our checks.

In the *Types & Grammar* title of this series, I explored another pattern that I slightly prefer:

```
var vals = [ "foo", "bar", 42, "baz" ];

if (~vals.indexOf( 42 )) {
    // found it!
}
```

The ~ operator here conforms the return value of `indexOf(..)` to a value range that is suitably boolean coercible. That is, -1 produces 0 (falsy), and anything else produces a nonzero (truthy) value, which is what we for deciding if we found the value or not.

While I think that's an improvement, others strongly disagree. However, no one can argue that `indexOf(..)`'s searching logic is perfect. It fails to find `NaN` values in the array, for example.

So a proposal has surfaced and gained a lot of support for adding a real boolean-returning array search method, called `includes(..)`:

```
var vals = [ "foo", "bar", 42, "baz" ];

if (vals.includes( 42 )) {
    // found it!
}
```

`Array#includes(..)` uses matching logic that will find `NaN` values, but will not distinguish between -0 and 0 (see the *Types & Grammar* title of this series). If you don't care about -0 values in your programs, this will likely be exactly what you're hoping for. If you *do* care about -0, you'll need to do your own searching logic, likely using the `Object.is(..)` utility (see Chapter 6).

SIMD

We cover Single Instruction, Multiple Data (SIMD) in more detail in the *Async & Performance* title of this series, but it bears a brief mention here, as it's one of the next likely features to land in a future JS.

The SIMD API exposes various low-level (CPU) instructions that can operate on more than a single number value at a time. For example, you'll be able to specify two *vectors* of 4 or 8 numbers each, and multiply the respective elements all at once (data parallelism!).

Consider:

```
var v1 = SIMD.float32x4( 3.14159, 21.0, 32.3, 55.55 );
var v2 = SIMD.float32x4( 2.1, 3.2, 4.3, 5.4 );

SIMD.float32x4.mul( v1, v2 );
// [ 6.597339, 67.2, 138.89, 299.97 ]
```

SIMD will include several other operations besides `mul(..)` (multiplication), such as `sub()`, `div()`, `abs()`, `neg()`, `sqrt()`, and many more.

Parallel math operations are critical for the next generations of high performance JS applications.

WebAssembly (WASM)

Brendan Eich made a late-breaking announcement near the completion of the first edition of this title that has the potential to significantly impact the future path of JavaScript: WebAssembly (WASM). We will not be able to cover WASM in detail here, as it's extremely early at the time of this writing. But this title would be incomplete without at least a brief mention of it.

One of the strongest pressures on the recent (and near future) design changes of the JS language has been the desire that it become a more suitable target for transpilation/cross-compilation from other languages (like C/C++, ClojureScript, etc.). Obviously, performance of code running as JavaScript has been a primary concern.

As discussed in the *Async & Performance* title of this series, a few years ago a group of developers at Mozilla introduced an idea to JavaScript called ASM.js. ASM.js is a subset of valid JS that most significantly restricts certain actions that make code hard for the JS engine to optimize. The result is that ASM.js-compatible code running in an ASM-aware engine can run remarkably faster, nearly on par with native optimized C equivalents. Many viewed ASM.js as the most likely backbone on which performance-hungry applications would ride in JavaScript.

In other words, all roads to running code in the browser *lead through JavaScript*.

That is, until the WASM announcement. WASM provides an alternate path for other languages to target the browser's runtime environment without having to first pass through JavaScript. Essentially, if WASM takes off, JS engines will gain an extra capability to execute a binary format of code that can be seen as somewhat similar to a bytecode (like that which runs on the JVM).

WASM proposes a format for a binary representation of a highly compressed AST (syntax tree) of code, which can then give instructions directly to the JS engine and its underpinnings, without having to be parsed by JS, or even behave by the rules of JS. Languages like C or C++ can be compiled directly to the WASM format instead of ASM.js, and gain an extra speed advantage by skipping the JS parsing.

The near term goal for WASM is to have parity with ASM.js and indeed JS. But eventually, it's expected that WASM will grow new capabilities that surpass anything JS could do. For example, the pressure for JS to evolve radical features like threads—a change that would certainly send major shockwaves through the JS ecosystem—has a more hopeful future as a future WASM extension, relieving the pressure to change JS.

In fact, this new roadmap opens up many new roads for many languages to target the web runtime. That's an exciting new future path for the web platform!

What does it mean for JS? Will JS become irrelevant or "die"? Absolutely not. ASM.js will likely not see much of a future beyond the next couple of years, but the majority of JS is quite safely anchored in the web platform story.

Proponents of WASM suggest its success will mean that the design of JS will be protected from pressures that would have eventually stretched it beyond assumed breaking points of reasonability. It is projected that WASM will become the preferred target for high-performance parts of applications, as authored in any of a myriad of different languages.

Interestingly, JavaScript is one of the languages less likely to target WASM in the future. There may be future changes that carve out subsets of JS that might be tenable for such targeting, but that path doesn't seem high on the priority list.

While JS likely won't be much of a WASM funnel, JS code and WASM code will be able to interoperate in the most significant ways, just as naturally as current module interactions. You can imagine calling a JS function like foo() and having that actually invoke a WASM function of that name with the power to run well outside the constraints of the rest of your JS.

Things that are currently written in JS will probably continue to always be written in JS, at least for the foreseeable future. Things that are transpiled to JS will probably eventually at least consider targeting WASM instead. For things that need the utmost in performance with minimal tolerance for layers of abstraction, the likely choice will be to find a suitable non-JS language to author in, and then targeting WASM.

There's a good chance that this shift will be slow, and will be years in the making. WASM landing in all the major browser platforms is probably a few years out at best. In the meantime, the WASM project (*https://github.com/WebAssembly*) has an early polyfill to demonstrate proof-of-concept for its basic tenets.

But as time goes on, and as WASM learns new non-JS tricks, it's not too much a stretch of imagination to see some currently-JS things being refactored to a WASM-targetable language. For example, the performance-sensitive parts of frameworks, game engines, and other heavily used tools might very well benefit from such a shift. Developers using these tools in their web applications likely won't notice much difference in usage or integration, but will just automatically take advantage of the performance and capabilities.

What's certain is that the more real WASM becomes over time, the more it means to the trajectory and design of JavaScript. It's perhaps one of the most important "beyond ES6" topics that developers should keep an eye on.

Review

If all the other books in this series essentially propose this challenge, "you (may) not know JS (as much as you thought)," this book has instead suggested, "you don't know JS anymore." The book has covered a ton of new stuff added to the language in ES6. It's an exciting collection of new language features and paradigms that will forever improve our JS programs.

But JS is not done with ES6! Not even close. There's already quite a few features in various stages of development for the "beyond ES6" timeframe. In this chapter, we briefly looked at some of the most likely candidates to land in JS very soon.

`async functions` are powerful syntactic sugar on top of the generators + promises pattern (see Chapter 4). `Object.observe(..)` adds direct native support for observing object change events, which is critical for implementing data binding. The `**` exponentiation operator, `...` for object properties, and `Array#includes(..)` are all simple but helpful improvements to existing mechanisms. Finally, SIMD ushers in a new era in the evolution of high-performance JS.

Cliché as it sounds, the future of JS is really bright! The challenge of this series, and indeed of this book, is incumbent on every reader now. What are you waiting for? It's time to get learning and exploring!

Acknowledgments

I have many people to thank for making this book title and the overall series happen.

First, I must thank my wife Christen Simpson, and my two kids Ethan and Emily, for putting up with Dad always pecking away at the computer. Even when not writing books, my obsession with JavaScript glues my eyes to the screen far more than it should. That time I borrow from my family is the reason these books can so deeply and completely explain JavaScript to you, the reader. I owe my family everything.

I'd like to thank my editors at O'Reilly, namely Simon St.Laurent and Brian MacDonald, as well as the rest of the editorial and marketing staff. They are fantastic to work with, and have been especially accommodating during this experiment into "open source" book writing, editing, and production.

Thank you to the many folks who have participated in making this book series better by providing editorial suggestions and corrections, including Shelley Powers, Tim Ferro, Evan Borden, Forrest L. Norvell, Jennifer Davis, Jesse Harlin, and many others. A big thank you to Rick Waldron for writing the Foreword for this title.

Thank you to the countless folks in the community, including members of the TC39 committee, who have shared so much knowledge with the rest of us, and especially tolerated my incessant questions and explorations with patience and detail. John-David Dalton, Juriy "kangax" Zaytsev, Mathias Bynens, Axel Rauschmayer, Nicholas

Zakas, Angus Croll, Reginald Braithwaite, Dave Herman, Brendan Eich, Allen Wirfs-Brock, Bradley Meck, Domenic Denicola, David Walsh, Tim Disney, Peter van der Zee, Andrea Giammarchi, Kit Cambridge, Eric Elliott, André Bargull, Caitlin Potter, Brian Terlson, Ingvar Stepanyan, Chris Dickinson, Luke Hoban, and so many others, I can't even scratch the surface.

The *You Don't Know JS* book series was born on Kickstarter, so I also wish to thank all my (nearly) 500 generous backers, without whom this book series could not have happened:

Jan Szpila, nokiko, Murali Krishnamoorthy, Ryan Joy, Craig Patchett, pdqtrader, Dale Fukami, ray hatfield, R0drigo Perez [Mx], Dan Petitt, Jack Franklin, Andrew Berry, Brian Grinstead, Rob Sutherland, Sergi Meseguer, Phillip Gourley, Mark Watson, Jeff Carouth, Alfredo Sumaran, Martin Sachse, Marcio Barrios, Dan, AimelyneM, Matt Sullivan, Delnatte Pierre-Antoine, Jake Smith, Eugen Tudorancea, Iris, David Trinh, simonstl, Ray Daly, Uros Gruber, Justin Myers, Shai Zonis, Mom & Dad, Devin Clark, Dennis Palmer, Brian Panahi Johnson, Josh Marshall, Marshall, Dennis Kerr, Matt Steele, Erik Slagter, Sacah, Justin Rainbow, Christian Nilsson, Delapouite, D.Pereira, Nicolas Hoizey, George V. Reilly, Dan Reeves, Bruno Laturner, Chad Jennings, Shane King, Jeremiah Lee Cohick, od3n, Stan Yamane, Marko Vucinic, Jim B, Stephen Collins, Ægir Þorsteinsson, Eric Pederson, Owain, Nathan Smith, Jeanetteurphy, Alexandre ELISÉ, Chris Peterson, Rik Watson, Luke Matthews, Justin Lowery, Morten Nielsen, Vernon Kesner, Chetan Shenoy, Paul Tregoing, Marc Grabanski, Dion Almaer, Andrew Sullivan, Keith Elsass, Tom Burke, Brian Ashenfelter, David Stuart, Karl Swedberg, Graeme, Brandon Hays, John Christopher, Gior, manoj reddy, Chad Smith, Jared Harbour, Minoru TODA, Chris Wigley, Daniel Mee, Mike, Handyface, Alex Jahraus, Carl Furrow, Rob Foulkrod, Max Shishkin, Leigh Penny Jr., Robert Ferguson, Mike van Hoenselaar, Hasse Schougaard, rajan venkataguru, Jeff Adams, Trae Robbins, Rolf Langenhuijzen, Jorge Antunes, Alex Koloskov, Hugh Greenish, Tim Jones, Jose Ochoa, Michael Brennan-White, Naga Harish Muvva, Barkóczi Dávid, Kitt Hodsden, Paul McGraw, Sascha Goldhofer, Andrew Metcalf, Markus Krogh, Michael Mathews, Matt Jared, Juanfran, Georgie Kirschner, Kenny Lee, Ted Zhang, Amit Pahwa, Inbal Sinai, Dan Raine, Schabse Laks, Michael Tervoort, Alexandre Abreu, Alan Joseph Williams, NicolasD, Cindy Wong, Reg Braithwaite, LocalPCGuy, Jon Friskics, Chris Merriman, John

Pena, Jacob Katz, Sue Lockwood, Magnus Johansson, Jeremy Crapsey, Grzegorz Pawłowski, nico nuzzaci, Christine Wilks, Hans Bergren, charles montgomery, Ariel בר-לבב Fogel, Ivan Kolev, Daniel Campos, Hugh Wood, Christian Bradford, Frédéric Harper, Ionuţ Dan Popa, Jeff Trimble, Rupert Wood, Trey Carrico, Pancho Lopez, Joël kuijten, Tom A Marra, Jeff Jewiss, Jacob Rios, Paolo Di Stefano, Soledad Penades, Chris Gerber, Andrey Dolganov, Wil Moore III, Thomas Martineau, Kareem, Ben Thouret, Udi Nir, Morgan Laupies, jory carson-burson, Nathan L Smith, Eric Damon Walters, Derry Lozano-Hoyland, Geoffrey Wiseman, mkeehner, KatieK, Scott MacFarlane, Brian LaShomb, Adrien Mas, christopher ross, Ian Littman, Dan Atkinson, Elliot Jobe, Nick Dozier, Peter Wooley, John Hoover, dan, Martin A. Jackson, Héctor Fernando Hurtado, andy ennamorato, Paul Seltmann, Melissa Gore, Dave Pollard, Jack Smith, Philip Da Silva, Guy Israeli, @megalithic, Damian Crawford, Felix Gliesche, April Carter Grant, Heidi, jim tierney, Andrea Giammarchi, Nico Vignola, Don Jones, Chris Hartjes, Alex Howes, john gibbon, David J. Groom, BBox, Yu *Dilys* Sun, Nate Steiner, Brandon Satrom, Brian Wyant, Wesley Hales, Ian Pouncey, Timothy Kevin Oxley, George Terezakis, sanjay raj, Jordan Harband, Marko McLion, Wolfgang Kaufmann, Pascal Peuckert, Dave Nugent, Markus Liebelt, Welling Guzman, Nick Cooley, Daniel Mesquita, Robert Syvarth, Chris Coyier, Rémy Bach, Adam Dougal, Alistair Duggin, David Loidolt, Ed Richer, Brian Chenault, GoldFire Studios, Carles Andrés, Carlos Cabo, Yuya Saito, roberto ricardo, Barnett Klane, Mike Moore, Kevin Marx, Justin Love, Joe Taylor, Paul Dijou, Michael Kohler, Rob Cassie, Mike Tierney, Cody Leroy Lindley, tofuji, Shimon Schwartz, Raymond, Luc De Brouwer, David Hayes, Rhys Brett-Bowen, Dmitry, Aziz Khoury, Dean, Scott Tolinski - Level Up, Clement Boirie, Djordje Lukic, Anton Kotenko, Rafael Corral, Philip Hurwitz, Jonathan Pidgeon, Jason Campbell, Joseph C., SwiftOne, Jan Hohner, Derick Bailey, getify, Daniel Cousineau, Chris Charlton, Eric Turner, David Turner, Joël Galeran, Dharma Vagabond, adam, Dirk van Bergen, dave ♥♪★ furf, Vedran Zakanj, Ryan McAllen, Natalie Patrice Tucker, Eric J. Bivona, Adam Spooner, Aaron Cavano, Kelly Packer, Eric J, Martin Drenovac, Emilis, Michael Pelikan, Scott F. Walter, Josh Freeman, Brandon Hudgeons, vijay chennupati, Bill Glennon, Robin R., Troy Forster, otaku_coder, Brad, Scott, Frederick Ostrander, Adam Brill, Seb Flippence, Michael Anderson, Jacob, Adam Randlett, Standard, Joshua Clanton, Sebastian Kouba, Chris Deck, SwordFire, Hannes Papenberg,

Richard Woeber, hnzz, Rob Crowther, Jedidiah Broadbent, Sergey Chernyshev, Jay-Ar Jamon, Ben Combee, luciano bonachela, Mark Tomlinson, Kit Cambridge, Michael Melgares, Jacob Adams, Adrian Bruinhout, Bev Wieber, Scott Puleo, Thomas Herzog, April Leone, Daniel Mizieliński, Kees van Ginkel, Jon Abrams, Erwin Heiser, Avi Laviad, David newell, Jean-Francois Turcot, Niko Roberts, Erik Dana, Charles Neill, Aaron Holmes, Grzegorz Ziółkowski, Nathan Youngman, Timothy, Jacob Mather, Michael Allan, Mohit Seth, Ryan Ewing, Benjamin Van Treese, Marcelo Santos, Denis Wolf, Phil Keys, Chris Yung, Timo Tijhof, Martin Lekvall, Agendine, Greg Whitworth, Helen Humphrey, Dougal Campbell, Johannes Harth, Bruno Girin, Brian Hough, Darren Newton, Craig McPheat, Olivier Tille, Dennis Roethig, Mathias Bynens, Brendan Stromberger, sundeep, John Meyer, Ron Male, John F Croston III, gigante, Carl Bergenhem, B.J. May, Rebekah Tyler, Ted Foxberry, Jordan Reese, Terry Suitor, afeliz, Tom Kiefer, Darragh Duffy, Kevin Vanderbeken, Andy Pearson, Simon Mac Donald, Abid Din, Chris Joel, Tomas Theunissen, David Dick, Paul Grock, Brandon Wood, John Weis, dgrebb, Nick Jenkins, Chuck Lane, Johnny Megahan, marzsman, Tatu Tamminen, Geoffrey Knauth, Alexander Tarmolov, Jeremy Tymes, Chad Auld, Sean Parmelee, Rob Staenke, Dan Bender, Yannick derwa, Joshua Jones, Geert Plaisier, Tom LeZotte, Christen Simpson, Stefan Bruvik, Justin Falcone, Carlos Santana, Michael Weiss, Pablo Villoslada, Peter deHaan, Dimitris Iliopoulos, seyDoggy, Adam Jordens, Noah Kantrowitz, Amol M, Matthew Winnard, Dirk Ginader, Phinam Bui, David Rapson, Andrew Baxter, Florian Bougel, Michael George, Alban Escalier, Daniel Sellers, Sasha Rudan, John Green, Robert Kowalski, David I. Teixeira (@ditma, Charles Carpenter, Justin Yost, Sam S, Denis Ciccale, Kevin Sheurs, Yannick Croissant, Pau Fracés, Stephen McGowan, Shawn Searcy, Chris Ruppel, Kevin Lamping, Jessica Campbell, Christopher Schmitt, Sablons, Jonathan Reisdorf, Bunni Gek, Teddy Huff, Michael Mullany, Michael Fürstenberg, Carl Henderson, Rick Yoesting, Scott Nichols, Hernán Ciudad, Andrew Maier, Mike Stapp, Jesse Shawl, Sérgio Lopes, jsulak, Shawn Price, Joel Clermont, Chris Ridmann, Sean Timm, Jason Finch, Aiden Montgomery, Elijah Manor, Derek Gathright, Jesse Harlin, Dillon Curry, Courtney Myers, Diego Cadenas, Arne de Bree, João Paulo Dubas, James Taylor, Philipp Kraeutli, Mihai Păun, Sam Gharegozlou, joshjs, Matt Murchison, Eric Windham, Timo Behrmann, Andrew Hall, joshua price, Théophile Villard

This book series is being produced in an open source fashion, including editing and production. We owe GitHub a debt of gratitude for making that sort of thing possible for the community!

Thank you again to all the countless folks I didn't name but who I nonetheless owe thanks. May this book series be "owned" by all of us and serve to contribute to increasing awareness and understanding of the JavaScript language, to the benefit of all current and future community contributors.

About the Author

Kyle Simpson is an Open Web Evangelist who's passionate about all things JavaScript. He's an author, workshop trainer, tech speaker, and OSS contributor/leader.

Colophon

The cover font for *ES6 & Beyond* is Interstate. The text font is Adobe Minion Pro; the heading font is Adobe Myriad Condensed; and the code font is Dalton Maag's Ubuntu Mono.

Get even more for your money.

Join the O'Reilly Community, and register the O'Reilly books you own. It's free, and you'll get:

- $4.99 ebook upgrade offer
- 40% upgrade offer on O'Reilly print books
- Membership discounts on books and events
- Free lifetime updates to ebooks and videos
- Multiple ebook formats, DRM FREE
- Participation in the O'Reilly community
- Newsletters
- Account management
- 100% Satisfaction Guarantee

Signing up is easy:

1. Go to: oreilly.com/go/register
2. Create an O'Reilly login.
3. Provide your address.
4. Register your books.

Note: English-language books only

To order books online:
oreilly.com/store

For questions about products or an order:
orders@oreilly.com

To sign up to get topic-specific email announcements and/or news about upcoming books, conferences, special offers, and new technologies:
elists@oreilly.com

For technical questions about book content:
booktech@oreilly.com

To submit new book proposals to our editors:
proposals@oreilly.com

O'Reilly books are available in multiple DRM-free ebook formats. For more information:
oreilly.com/ebooks

Lightning Source UK Ltd.
Milton Keynes UK
UKOW05f1023300916

284168UK00005B/18/P